CRITICAL ESSAYS
ON AYN RAND'S
THE FOUNTAINHEAD

EMRE GURGEN

authorHOUSE

AuthorHouse™
1663 Liberty Drive
Bloomington, IN 47403
www.authorhouse.com
Phone: 833-262-8899

Published by AuthorHouse 08/12/2022

ISBN: 978-1-6655-6688-9 (sc)
ISBN: 978-1-6655-6689-6 (hc)
ISBN: 978-1-6655-6687-2 (e)

Library of Congress Control Number: 2022914051

Print information available on the last page.

Any people depicted in stock imagery provided by Getty Images are models, and such images are being used for illustrative purposes only. Certain stock imagery © Getty Images.

This book is printed on acid-free paper.

Because of the dynamic nature of the Internet, any web addresses or links contained in this book may have changed since publication and may no longer be valid. The views expressed in this work are solely those of the author and do not necessarily reflect the views of the publisher, and the publisher hereby disclaims any responsibility for them.

707-4

707-19

CONTENTS

INTRODUCTION

I wrote this *Fountainhead* essay book for students of *Objectivism*, fans of Ayn Rand, or simply for people who are interested in pondering the novel's unorthodox ideas. As such, this essay book shows readers 3 things: how *the Fountainhead* expresses American values and what this means for characters who embrace first-handed principles; how the novel elevates principles of capitalism and individualism over the ideology of collectivism and communism and how this shapes civilization; and, finally, how Howard Roark, the book's hero-protagonist, energizes a variety of characters in the novel by living out who he is.

To help people understand the novel better, I also published a *Fountainhead Reference Guide*, about a year ago, which is a companion to both *the Fountainhead* and this essay book. A sample of this study guide, and links to it, can be found on my personal author website: www.aynrandanalyzed.com.

ESSAY 1

How *The Fountainhead* Expresses America's Founding Values

The Fountainhead is the **greatest American novel of all time**: since it links the creative spirit of Americans to the progress of human civilization. The book does this by showing readers that "human beings [advance] because of the efforts of people who are not second handers" (Den Uyl, 66). Creators, innovators, and discovers, who move society forward—who fuel the engine of progress—because "they follow their own ideas and insights [instead] of rely[ing] on what others think and believe" (Den Uyl, 92). People who give progress to the human species—who advance humankind—by showing us that "at the essential level innovation is what is critical to moving life forward" (Den Uyl, 99). Since transformation, or transcending where we are to something greater and better, is central to both America and *The Fountainhead*. For this reason, the novel's hero-protagonist, Roark, is "the embodiment of the correct theory of [American] human progress" (Den Uyl, 61).

Specifically, *the Fountainhead* is a novel that depicts the meaning of American individualism. For "Howard Roark is a brilliant young architect uninterested in re-creating the past. Rather, he wishes to build according to his own plans and specifications" (Den Uyl, 31). Thus, the opinions of others, including that of most other architects, do not matter to him. For Roark is an individual who makes advances by living according to his own individual truth and vision. Ergo, Roark's spirit ultimately shows readers that innovation and advancement come from the one who breaks away from the crowd and lives by a new vision. Since "ideas are what move the world, and while they can be shared, they originate and are advanced by individuals" (Den Uyl, 61).

Judging by the overwhelming response *The Fountainhead* received from members of the reading public, "not by the public as an organized *collective*—but by single individual readers who discovered it of their own choice, who read it on their own initiative and recommended it on their own judgment"—it is reasonable to say that that *The Fountainhead* connected to their sense of what it means to be an American (Berliner, 673). Accordingly, many Americans lauded the American values the novel stands for. Thus, soldiers from all marshal-ranks praised *The Fountainhead* independently, ordinary fans from all backgrounds acclaimed the book autonomously, businessmen from all social strata commended the novel impartially. For they all felt that *The Fountainhead* either justified why they fought, or inspired them to achieve in their own lives, or aligned with their professional goals somehow.

For example, Americans soldiers, from different marshal ranks—i.e. cadets, privates, airmen, lieutenants, and enlisted men—were so moved by *The Fountainhead* that they "eagerly passed [the book] from reader to reader" not only because the novel justified "U.S. involvement" in World "War" II[1] by "providing a welcome [explanation] on the reasons for U.S. involvement in the war" but also because it stimulated their minds, as well. (Burns, 92). As one trooper put it:

> *The Fountainhead made me realize that we fight to protect American values (i.e. civil liberties) from the encroachments of the evil axis powers, who together are trying to make me a slave, by depriving me of my freedom, seizing my person, taking my home and property, and stripping my family of their sovereign rights as individual human beings*

Evidently, this soldier fully realized, after reading *The Fountainhead*, that he risked his life, in World War II, to safeguard his right to think freely, speak freely, and live freely, in a free country. Besides justifying the

---

[1] For Rand, "war, especially World War II, is an example of what happens when one looks to the state rather than to trade and cooperation among individuals as the means to social order, prosperity, and peaceful coexistence. [Since] war, the quintessential collective effort in practice, [is] for Rand the *result* of certain principles rather than a statement of them." (Den Uyl, 5).

military's right to defend their lives, protect their families, and safeguard their property – in a just war – against the encroachments of a foreign hegemon, *The Fountainhead* was "a hot commodity among military units" because it provided welcome moral instruction (Burns, 92). For soldiers could take their minds off of the *Great War* for a while—off of trench warfare for a bit—by immersing themselves in a fictional world where their imaginations could roam free. This is why troopers "eagerly passed [*The Fountainhead*] from reader to reader," so they could relieve "their boredom" by giving their "brains some well needed exercise" (Burns, 92). Indeed, Ayn Rand especially enjoyed the many letters she received from men in the armed forces. [For] she recalled letters from flyers who told her that after every mission they would gather around a candle and read passages from *The Fountainhead*. One soldier [even] said that he would have felt much better if he thought that the war was being fought for the ideals of *The Fountainhead*." (Ralston, 72).

Besides stimulating soldiers, many ordinary fans also thought that *The Fountainhead* was a great work of "American literature" (Berliner, 315). Because the novel not only "helped [them clarify] their views on life [thereby giving them aid] in [their moral] decisions," but, most importantly, because it provided solace "when [they] felt unhappy" (Berliner, 235). Other admirers who were "just going to college [read *The Fountainhead* to equip themselves] with the [book's] ideals" as intellectual ammunition against their forthcoming collectivist college years. (Berliner, 315). Other Americans also liked *the Fountainhead*, since they "wanted to choose a profession" that meant as much to them as "writing" the *Fountainhead* did to Ayn Rand (Berliner, 340). Still others were attracted to *The Fountainhead* because they were "individualist" writers who wanted emotional fuel to help them *not* feel so "intellectually lonely" (Berliner, 389). Since they were minority voices who were in "complete sympathy with [Ayn Rand's] ideas on individualism" (Berliner, 389). This is why many people told Ayn Rand that *The Fountainhead* was to them "in the nature of a revelation [of their values] and reaffirmation" of themselves: since her book encouraged Americans to fully "discard [the] doctrine of [altruism and] self-sacrifice as an ideal, [so they could find] a different positive faith in humanity" (Berliner, 91, 80). Finally, many Americans read *The Fountainhead* because they wanted to know where Ayn Rand drew her ideological " 'strength' " from (Berliner, 97).

Judging by the thousands of enthusiastic letters Ayn Rand received from Americans in response to *The Fountainhead*, it is clear that her book affirmed people's basic American drive towards individualism and self-actualization. Others even offered their financial assistance.

For example, many American businessmen were so touched by Ayn Rand's book that they either offered their own money to advertise her novel, or were willing to spend their own funds to put-up billboards supporting her book, or wanted to name their businesses after her work. For example, a "fishing tackle" maker offered to finance *Fountainhead* advertisements from his own pocket, because the novel defended his right to make just profits. (Berliner, 94). Another businessman erected signs advertising *The Fountainhead*, since he wanted to spread an ideology that supported his ability to prosper. A motel owner named his roadhouse *The Fountainhead* to increase his profits over time by linking the values of his businesses to the positive philosophy of *The Fountainhead*.

Further, many elite Americans wrote poignant missives to Ayn Rand, because they felt that her book either supported their work ethic, or defended their stance against collectivism, or railed against the tyranny of the masses, or activated their values in some other way. For example, Tom Girdler, founder and chairman of *Republic Steel and Vultee Aircraft*, was so inspired by Ayn Rand's portrait of hardworking Americans that he sent her "galleys of [his] book *The Right to Work.*" (Berliner, 81). Similarly, Samuel B. Pettingill, an individualist congressman from Indiana, wrote an article in the "Harford Times," supporting *The Fountainhead* since it portrayed an image of a man who went against and defeated the principles of collectivism. (Berliner, 76). John C. Gall, a prominent conservative attorney, wrote Ayn Rand a moving "reader's response" to *The Fountainhead*, in which he praised her brave stand against illiberal socialist democracies, like the governments of *Soviet Russia* (Berliner, 78).

The spirit of Howard Roark also found a response among writers, journalists, screenwriters, novelists, literary agents, critics, and artists, who all wrote Ayn Rand enthusiastic letters expressing their admiration for her fictional hero.

In sum, by buying and reading *The Fountainhead*, the American "public" helped make the book a financial success, "against the opposition of the intellectual Toohey's" (Berliner, 228).

For Americans not only appreciated Ayn Rand's direct portrayal of how the real world actually works but respected her seering honesty as well.

Evidently, Americans where unafraid of liking, praising, and defending *The Fountainhead*, since they were ready for a clear novel, with bold views, that safeguarded their right to be different. For many Americans were sick-and-tired "of halfhearted evasions, [floating] generalities, [unprincipled] compromises, standard [euphemisms] and feeble attempts to please everybody" both in life and in fiction (Berliner, 244). Rather, they wanted a book that told them the truth directly. A novel that was full of bold ideological statements. A book that did not sugar coat unpleasant truths with cloying bromides or inoffensive speech. But a novel that was unafraid to hurt people's feelings. Happily, they got what they wanted in *The Fountainhead*. For American readers found in the book a new set of values that overrode the bleak, nihilistic dreariness, of our modern age—(i.e. the "sterile, hopeless, cynicism of" contemporary civilization) (Rand, Journals, 81). For *the Fountainhead* shows readers that "*Individualism*, in all its deepest meaning and implications, such as has never been preached before: individualism of the spirit, of ethics, and of philosophy, and not merely individualism as an economic practice," is fundamentally good (Rand, Journals, 81). That, conversely, the ultimate consequences of collective group-think (i.e. communism) is stagnation.

Further, Ayn Rand illustrates in *The Fountainhead* that individualism does not just apply to the "good old *rugged individualism* of small shopkeepers [but] individualism also applies to a man's soul" (Rand, Journals, 81). For individualism, the book shows, is also a moral code, a religion, and an organizing principle, that prompts men to act as they should. Both in their personal lives and in their relationships with each other. Since the book emphasizes the concept that each person is a *sovereign* individual with a self-made soul.

Evidently, because Americans liked Ayn Rand's message of individualism so much, they ultimately made *The Fountainhead* successful by buying it. For Americans thought that Ayn "Rand gave voice to values, like individualism [selfishness, and egoism] that were not getting expression elsewhere in the literary, artistic, or political world" (Den Uyl, 14). Thus they told each other to buy the novel *not* because it was a form of escapist entertainment. But because it provided valuable moral instruction on how they could live a happy life. By leading a purpose-driven reality. Clearly, because most Americans strongly approved of Ayn Rand and her ideas, *The Fountainhead* trickled-up to widespread reader acclaim "through sheer, genuine popular response" (Berliner, 244). Despite the heinous censure of the so-called intelligentsia. Ergo, despite being rejected by 12 publishers on grounds that it would not sell because it was 'too intellectual,' 'too literary,' 'too unconventional,' 'too strong' 'not human' enough, and too 'unsympathetic," the book sold evermore—daily, weekly, monthly, and yearly—until it became a best-seller (Berliner, 103, 244, 628, 673, 75). For Americans needed a Howard Roark like figure, who expressed, in human-and-particular terms, their highest aspirations as men. Accordingly, sales of AR's book increased daily thanks to "a steady, growing, voluntary [grassroots] campaign" consisting of word-of-mouth publicity (Berliner, 228, 244, 228). This word-of-mouth buzz, in turn, resulted in a "serialized [graphic] strip," of *The Fountainhead* being published in the "Hearst Papers" (Berliner, 228). This hubbub also generated many "popular reprints" (Berliner, 241). Thus, thanks to the American public's overwhelming appreciation of *The Fountainhead*, the book ultimately placed highly on all the bestseller lists. Not because it was well marketed and advertised (it wasn't) but because Americans were starved to read a book that connected to their sense of telling the truth directly; not evading reality. For Americans found in *The Fountainhead* a novel that was good, and knew it, and did not apologize for it.

International readers also demanded to read *The Fountainhead* in their own countries and languages, since foreigners—especially people who shared America's values—clamored for a translation in their native tongues. So they could better understand what Ayn Rand wrote and why. Such a foreign call for Ayn Rand's straight-talk resulted in *The*

Fountainhead being translated into 25 languages—Albanian; Bulgarian; Chinese; Croatian; Chezch; Danish; Dutch; French; German; Greek; Hebrew; Icelandic; Italian; Japanese; Mongolia; Norwegian; Polish; Portuguese; Romanian; Russian; Slovakian; Spanish; Swedish; Turkish; and Ukrainian. Strong global demand for the book also lead to "more than 6.5 million copies of *The Novel* [selling] worldwide" ("The Fountainhead," n.d.). Indeed, *The Fountainhead* has been translated, so widely, and has been sold, so broadly, precisely because it expresses to people all over the world what Americans feel in spirit but cannot articulate for themselves (i.e. that *proper* selfish is good, that *improper* selflessness is bad). In other words, strong worldwide sales of *The Fountainhead* proves that Ayn Rand's book links to who people are at a fundamental level, whether they are Americans, or not.

Indeed, since the novel features many free-thinking, hard-working, Americans who flourish in many different professions, it drew a passionate response from many American readers. Since members of the American public were starved to read serious literature, about many different characters, from all walks-of-life, eventually succeeding, despite initial set-backs, frustrations, and failures. In this sense, *The Fountainhead* gave everyday Americans precisely the sort of spiritual-fuel they needed to succeed in their own lives. Because the book concretizes the idea that people should pursue their own goals, realize their own aims, and achieve their own happiness, by being true to who they are deep down. Just like many characters in *the Fountainhead* are.

Also, by taking her case "for the inalienable rights of the creative individual to court, where a jury of twelve free-thinking Americans takes [Roark's] side" Ayn Rand shows us that Americans, like Roark, "pursue their own goals, seek their own happiness," and live their own lives, even if "millions of people" disagree (Heller, 107; Bernstein, 85). For the average American, to Ayn Rand, is a volitionally sovereign individual who characteristically makes-up his own mind about people, situations, and events. According to facts, evidence, and logical inference. Not someone who succumbs to sympathy for poor slum dwellers. Thus, because Ayn Rand believes that objective impartiality should rule the American justice system, she has her hero-protagonist (Roark) select a "tough-looking" jury comprised of "two executives of industry, two engineers, a mathematician, a truck driver, a bricklayer, an electrician, a gardener, and three factory workers" (Burns, 84; 707). Hard-working Americans who are united **not** by their ranks, their incomes, nor their blind sympathy for unfortunates. But Americans who think for themselves, value for themselves, feel for themselves, and judge for themselves, despite what others think. Even if the public disagrees. Because they have rational minds. Thus, these dozen American jurors do not yield to popular loathing of Roark whipped-up by a snarling public bent on destroying him. Rather, these honest American jurors independently conceive the truth about Roark objectively on their own.

Indeed, because these American jurors autonomously judge Roark despite what the crowd thinks, they *all* conclude that he deserves to be paid and valued for his work, just like they do. Ergo, they deliver Roark justice because they recognize the rightness of his cause. They recognize the rightness of his cause because they appreciate Roark's great worth as a human being. This objective sense of fairness, in turn, appeals to Roark's sense of justice. For it is the jury's method of using dispassionate reason to first identify reality; then to devise a reasonable action plan going forward, that Roark likes. For their "hard faces" tells Roark that these Americans will not subvert their better judgment for the malice of others (707). Just the reverse. Their creased faces show Roark that these jurors will be fair to him, since they are his sort of men: rational men and women who also use logic, just like he does, to think, understand, and form their own judgments. For Roark only trusts objective people to listen to him fairly and impartially. People who have not made-up their mind about his guilt, or innocence, in advance.

This, then, is one-way Rand democratizes her vision of firm justice through *juris prudence*. Another way she defends her love of American truth telling is by showing readers that it is these American jurors' sense of American Patriotism that qualifies them to judge Roark. That makes them worthy to partake in his trial.

Accordingly, Roark selects twelve U.S. citizens who favor the American principles he will express in his speech—"life, liberty, and the pursuit of happiness" (Cato, 9). Twelve patriotic jurors who are loyal to what America really is at heart. A land where people are free to work, act, think, and behave, according to their own best judgment, without undue governmental, social, and interpersonal interference. A land where inalienable individual rights flourish. Ergo, since Roark appeals to American values [2] to clear him of any wrong doing, the jury likes his support of creators throughout history—men who stood alone, thought for themselves and invented products that improved their own lives. For Roark speech not only shows this American jury that they should be rewarded for their own creations but Roark's speech "is successful because it asks the jurors to rediscover their own Americanness (Den Uyl, 106). To "search their [own] consciences for the truth that lies within them." (Den Uyl, 105). Thus, these jurors acquit Roark because he appeals to what they all know America to really be about, deep down inside. For "it would be hard to imagine anything other than an American jury being moved by [Roark's speech] because it would be hard to imagine anything but an American jury taking individualism so seriously." (Den Uyl, 106). Ergo, the jurors acquit Roark because they are Americans who see that it is American values to which Roark appeals. As such, the jury's "not guilty" verdict "proves critical [in] helping [Ayn Rand] reaffirm the basic wisdom of free-thinking independent Americans" (Burns, 84).

Indeed, Roark chooses 12 rational American souls to judge him—twelve independent American thinkers to decide his fate—since Roark's acquittal by a dozen of his moral peers shows readers that ordinary Americans like Roark. Because they share his ethical compass. For if the *Cortlandt* jurors lacked Roark's moral orientation they would not have exculpated him. But they release Roark because they also want to live in a free nation where they too are paid for their work. Where they too can benefit from their own creations, however modest, or extraordinary,

---

[2]   Evidently, Roark appeals to American values to acquit him by saying: "Now observe the results of a society built on the principle of individualism. This, our country. The noblest country in the history of men. The country of greatest achievement, greatest prosperity, greatest freedom. This country was not based on selfless service, sacrifice, renunciation or any precept of altruism. It was based on a man's right to the pursuit of happiness. His own happiness. Not anyone else's. A private, personal, selfish motive. Look at the results. Look at your own conscience" (715).

those creations are. In sum, Roark's independent stand, as articulated in his courtroom speech, about the sanctity of the creative mind, not only shows readers how a creative American lifestyle aligns with basic American values but Roark's speech also causes the jury to immediately see the justness of his cause. Thus, the jury unanimously acquits Roark, after *only* a few minutes, *without* really deliberating much, because the truth of his speech is self-evident. It needs no debate. Most importantly, Roark's immediate exoneration by his fellows suggests Ayn Rand's basic thesis that ultimately Americans want the paths of all creators to be cleared: whether they are grand geniuses, like a Howard Roark, or simply moral men and women, who share his inventive spirit.

In sum, through these jurors Rand shows us that she has great respect for the basic sense of justice and humanity of regular Americans. For their sense of justice is what brings normal American readers into the book and connects them to someone like a Howard Roark. Also, by having an American jury free Roark, Ayn Rand shows readers that "The American public is very wise" (Rand, Answers, 54). For it is the ordinary American who helps Roark win his court battle by voting "not guilty" at his trial.

Ergo, the acquittal of Roark during his *Cortlandt* trial is one-way Ayn Rand expresses her admiration for the great American spirit.

Another way Ayn Rand expresses her respect for regular Americans is by depicting an able construction worker named Mike Donnigan to be the best of everyman.

Mike Donnigan is an average moral American—a plain workman—who shares Roark's competent spirit. For he is the best of everyman, who brings out his own greatness, by building with Roark on many different construction projects. Whether it is large summer resort, like *Monadnock Valley*, or a small construction job, like *The Heller House*, Mike follows Roark to the ends of the earth. To create unique buildings with him. For Mike is drawn to Roark like an angel needs light, since working with Roark, on a series of great buildings, enables Mike to be true to himself. So he can realize the best within him. Thus, to draw out that noble part of his soul, Mike travels around the country in his "ancient Ford" truck building how he wants to build with Roark (86).

Indeed, since Mike becomes all he can be by working with Roark, he illuminates the American spirit of self-actualization. The American ethical theory of life which says that the highest good for man consists in realizing and fulfilling his full potential, so he can actualize his ideal or real self. Ergo, Donnigan learns to be even truer to himself by working with Roark on a sequence of matchless structures. For constructing magnificent buildings with Roark imbues Mike with an exulted feeling of pride and accomplishment for the great creative work he can do.

Above all, Mike proves that he is a real American man, with real American values, since he admires other competent Americans, like Roark, who are also good at their careers. Individuals, who also shine at their jobs. People who also work smart-and-hard (just like Mike does) in their chosen professions. Thus, whether Americans are janitors, who clean proficiently, or physicists, who define nature expertly, Mike admires them. For Mike "worships expertness of any kind," especially in construction (86). Particularly in the building trades. Therefore, Mike is awed when he sees Roark torch a perfect hole in a beam to insert a copper pipe through it. Mike is also impressed when he sees Roark "walk on narrow planks; on naked beams; [thousands of feet in the sky] as easily as the best of them" (84). Since these twin-acts convinces Mike that Roark is a competent construction worker who also has a bold spirit, just like he does. Thus, when Mike learns that Roark is not merely a superlative arc-welder and construction worker (like he is) but that Roark is also a college educated architect (like he is not) he is stunned. For Mike marvels that Roark is an educated architect who can correct his cite supervisor. Mike also appreciates that Roark is his own person, who knows his own mind, since Mike is also a unique individual, with his own distinctive being.

To explain, Mike is a distinct American man who defines his identity for himself; *not* a needy member of a construction guild who defines his identity tribally. For example, instead of opining in conformist agreement with other construction workers, Mike uses his mind, to the best of his ability, to evaluate people, situations, and events, objectively. According to facts, evidence, and proofs related to them. This is why Mike disbelieves his supervisor's opinion that Roark is a "stuck-up, stubborn, lousy bastard," since this view contradicts what Mike has seen for himself (86). Namely, that Roark forges friendships with his fellow co-workers *not* because they are rich, or powerful, or well-connected. But because they can help him build better. For Roark befriends people who love their work, are competent at what they do, and add value to his creations. Even if they are poor blue-collared workers. Mike realizes this because Mike relaxes with Roark in a basement speak-easy, after a hard day's work, drinking beers and swapping construction stories. At this bar, Mike tells Roark "his favorite tale of how he had fallen five stories when a scaffolding gave way under him; [and] Roark speaks of his days in the building trades" (86). If Roark thought it beneath him to befriend a working man who shares his passion for building he would *not* have gone to a pub with Mike. But he does. And Mike loves him for it. For Mike realizes that Roark does not judge people based on the contents of their wallets. But rather that Roark judge's people based on the contents of their characters.

Indeed, Mike's willingness to rely on observational evidence to form his own judgments, shows readers that Mike is not a mindless automaton, who robotically agrees with the evaluations of his superiors. Rather, Mike questions his bosses, if they make irrational statements that contradict what he has seen for himself. For Mike trusts his own eyes to gather the information he needs to evaluate people for who they really are. Even if his appraisals differ from what other builders think. This is why Mike realizes that his boss only says that Roark is conceited *not* because Roark is. But because Roark tells this man how to do his job better. For Roark will not sacrifice his better architectural judgment for Mike's supervisor's worse architectural directions. Mike realizes this because Mike is a free-thinking American man who judges other men, independently, even if everyone else disagrees. Ergo, Mike is a model American citizen who does not passively agree, or quietly assent, with his supervisor's opinions just because he is his boss. Rather, Mike is a self-governing American individual who questions his boss's judgement if his boss makes irrational claims that belie the reality of a person or situation.

In sum, Mike's admiration for "expertness of any kind," coupled with his respect for "other single-track devotions," makes Mike a quintessential American (86).

The Fountainhead also expresses the American concept of a merit-based – socially mobile – *Republican* civilization. A federated form of government, if you will, based on capitalism, where people who are good at what they do – perhaps even the best at what they do – rise-up in this world. A nation where individuals can better themselves; advance their living situations; and improve their lives, by applying creative thinking, to prodigious amounts of industry, in any practical field of endeavor. So they can rise to the commanding heights of civilization—monetarily, intellectually, emotionally, and physically—on their own volition. Because of what they do. By using their minds, then deploying their muscles, to master their occupations.

One example of this American self-made man (i.e. a *homo economicus* who rises in life by working smart-and-hard) is a businessman named Roger Enright. Roger Enright pulls himself out of the muck of poverty by focusing his mind on making money. For although Roger "start[s] life as a coal miner in Pennsylvania" eventually he climbs out of the bowels of the earth by saving a modest capital sum (174). Then Roger invests his modest savings in a small "oil concern," which he eventually turns into a thriving "oil business," with him in sole charge (174, 256). Eventually, Roger makes enough money from this oil business to create seven more companies: "a publishing house, a restaurant, a radio shop, a garage, a plant manufacturing electric refrigerators" an apartment building called *The Enright House*, and a private housing project called *Cortlandt Homes* (256). To build these businesses Enright "works twelve hours a day," with "ferocious energy, coining money where nobody else thought it would grow" (256, 258).

But occasionally Enright does fail [3]. Yet Enright does not get discouraged by his failures. Since when Enright is wrong he learns

---

[3] To learn how failure leads to success, please see **Failure: A Secret Strategy for Success. Part 1. Philosophy for Flourishing Episode 9 [U-Tube Video File]**. Retrieved from https://www.youtube.com/watch?v=JQIlk_h0S2o&t=45s by Biddle, C. (2020, July 29).

what he has to do the next time around to succeed. What knowledge, experience, and skills he needs to be successful, later. In the future. For Enright's method of creating successful businesses is iterative. If one of his business's tanks, Enright does not give up. He does not give in. He persists. He modifies how he operates. He refines his business models. He keeps at it until he gets it right. So the next time around he creates a business that succeeds. In other words, instead of internalizing his failures by letting his failures undercut his identity and self-esteem—i.e. doubting himself because he failed—Enright "get[s] out in the world, go[es] for things, sees what happens, deal[s] with the experience of failure, deal[s] with the experience of success, and learns from that sort of trial and error, iterative approach." (Biddle). In this way, Enright not only learns that his failures are ultimately a part of his success—steps on the way to his success—but that his commercial failure, if taken in the right spirit, can inspire him to excel. Can teach him what works by learning through business what does not. Thus, Enright embraces his professional mistakes as self-teaching moments that show him what not to do. So he can learn what to. This, then, is how Enright's failures are ultimately stepping stones that pave the way to the road of his final success. Because he uses his failures as launching points, for his final ascent to triumph. Thus, Enright "fail[s] and [is] proud of [his] failures," because they not only signal to him that he is "trying," but they also show him that his success is becoming more probable, likely, plausible (Biddle, ?). For Enright believes that to take any sort of action in this world to create any business whatsoever, he must fail, and enjoy his failures. Since his failures ultimately leads to his success, especially if he analyzes why he failed, so he does not fail again. Because success, in anything, Enright's life story shows, only comes after instances of unsuccess. Since making mistakes is part of the creative process that enables men like Enright to move forward with their vision. Conversely, if Enright was petrified of making an error, he would not be able to create any sort of business whatsoever. Because, "Success is a process. Life is a process. Living fully is a process. And you either embrace that [process]. And take everything that comes with it. Or you never try anything and you don't grow." (Biddle). Thus, because Enright is not afraid to fail he takes the calculated risks necessary succeed. Ergo, Enright's failures are not so bad. They are good. Because they teach him how to not fail again. How to be successful the next time at bat. For Enright sees his failures as self-correcting experiences. Thus, Enright does not feel sorry for himself because one of his company's botched. Rather, he moves on. He bounces back. He learns from his mistakes.

Yet, most of the time, Enright succeeds in business by first studying the field he is going to enter for a long time. Then, once he has researched the field thoroughly, Enright creates a sound business plan, a realistic mission statement, a practical operating plan, a viable marketing policy, a lucrative sales strategy, an efficient management structure, and a plausible target market. Thus, instead of being "risk adverse, [Enright] takes his most ambitious and exciting goals and strives to achieve them" (Biddle, 4:15-4:23).

And with each new business success Enright's self-confidence grows in his ability to make money. Since to earn "the millions he now own[s], no one had ever helped him." (256). Neither by giving value but not receiving value in return, nor by buying or selling "a share [of stock] in any of his enterprises" (256). For Roger never takes his companies public. Because Roger needs complete decisional freedom to act on his own business acumen. For Enright's business style (i.e. how he coins money in the business world) requires that he is completely free from all external trammels (i.e. from the interference of others). So he can fully profit from his mind. So he can reach a state of spiritual perfection by making money.

Thus, Roger achieves a joyous state-of-life by being an exemplar American businessman. A commercial value incarnate who brings commercial values to others. He does this by maintaining complete control over his businesses. Thus, Enright does not sell shares of his companies on the *New York Stock Exchange*. For he does not want business amateurs with worse business judgment telling a businessman expert with better business judgment what to do. For Roger alone has the creative mind, the firm will-power, the bold enterprise, and the commercial knowledge, to create flourishing businesses in the first place. In his professional line of endeavor. Thus, Enright does not want a CEO, a CFO, a COO [4], a Treasurer, shareholders, or anyone else telling him what to do. Instead, Enright is a solo-preneur, who cannot be limited by people telling him to do this, not that, so that this can result. Because if he implemented people's suggestions, Enright's companies would either likely fail, thereby causing him to become poor again. Or, conversely, his businesses would not be as successful as they could be, with him in full charge. With him as the sole leader. For Enright cannot have a situation where his businesses fail *not* because of something he did or did not do. But because of another person's mistakes. Since he would rather fall-or-rise, sink-or-swim, on his own. Due to what he has, or has not, done. Thus, to form, maintain, and operate his businesses, so they create just profits for all involved, Roger does not take his companies public. So he is not hampered by other people. For Enright cannot have other people make him poor again by yielding to their well-intentioned, though wholly misguided, business suggestions. Because to be a successful businessman, Roger knows that he must have a complete free hand to run his businesses himself. As he sees fit. Without an executive board telling him what to do. Without inexperienced people telling an experienced businessman how he should run his companies and why. Thus, because Enright does not want to diminish his ability to run his companies by getting the permission of less knowledgeable others for everything he does, he simply gives orders to his competent subordinates (i.e. his business managers) which they later implement. For Roger alone knows what actions his companies must take (i.e. how they should be run and why) so that profits accrue to all involved: Enright, first-and-foremost, since he originated these successful companies; his helpers, second-and-second most, because his employees helped him implement the firm's values; and his customers, third-and-third most, who improve

---

[4]   Though corporations actually enhance many people's lives—both individuals who form and operate them and individuals who buy goods and services from them—Roger Enright's personality requires that he form, own, and operate, his own businesses, with a total free hand. For Enright can only flourish if he is in exclusive charge of a perfect business hierarchy. Thus, he cannot be hogtied (i.e. hamstrung) by a corporation's executive board. For even though Roger recognizes that corporations are good for many people, Enright feels he can only be successful if he decides how his companies are run by himself. With him in total control of everything. This is who he is. And, that is fine.

their lives by purchasing his valuable goods and services. Thus, with each new business success Enright's commercial confidence grows (i.e. his industrial judgment becomes more accurate) since the steady rise of his businesses advances his ultimate trade success. This, then, is how Enright realizes his full potential. How Roger becomes his best self.

Further, Enright's characterization shows readers that since self-actualization is the goal of all Americans—because all American's want to realize their ideal, or real selves, by being true to who they are—Enright's particular path of being true to himself is through business. By exercising his business acumen. Thus, to be true to himself, Enright creates 7 successful companies that enable him to realize his American drive to better himself. For Enright's dynamic personality requires that he always strive to better his financial position, instead of resting on his laurels. Instead of relying on his previous business successes to live a comfortable life. Thus, Enright always actively pursues his goals instead of passively becoming a retired creature who reacts to the markets. For Enright must succeed evermore by challenging himself daily to excel.

Ergo, Enright's relentless drive to realize his business aims not only enables him to make his own life better but helps him improve his customers lives as well. By bringing his clients tangible material values (i.e. principled goods and services) that they need. For example, authors give Enright a percentage of their book sales, since his "publishing house" prints and illustrates their books, distributes and markets their books, then reprints and edits those books, for subsequent reissue (256). Hungry people buy meals from Enright's "restaurant" since foodies eat good fare at his diner at a fair price (256). Radio enthusiasts buy radios from Enright's "radio shop," since his stereos air information they need, or like, such as news, music, or sports. (256). Drivers frequent Enright's "garage," since his auto-shop fixes and services their vehicles at an affordable price, so they can maintain, even improve, their automobiles (256). Consumers buy Enright's "refrigerator[s]," since his refrigerators permit people to cool and freeze their comestibles, without using a messy icebox (256). People buy apartments in Roger's *Enright House*, so they can live "in sane comfort" (316). So they can benefit from Roger's "bright and bold" new building (272).

In sum, because Enright creates 7 different businesses that deliver sundry values to distinct people with marketplace efficiency, he is ultimately rewarded by the purchasing power of individual market actors, who collectively make him rich. Who together make discrete economic decisions one-by-one in a free marketplace of goods and services.

Ergo, by acting on his own business judgment in a *laissez affair* economy, Roger becomes a self-made multi-millionaire who transcends his childhood poverty to achieve life-success. For, despite his early poverty, Roger rises to business success by using his excellent commercial judgment to create a variety of successful enterprises. Companies that fulfill a valuable need in people's lives by providing beneficial goods and services at an affordable price. This, then, is how Enright realizes his full-potential. How Enright makes his American dream an American reality.

In sum, since making yourself an honest financial success is highly respected by Americans, American capitalists share Enright's commercial spirit of bettering their lives through free enterprise. But American capitalists are not the only individuals who appreciate Enright. Blue collared workers also like him. Since Enright shows regular workers that they too can rise-up in life. That they too can reach their highest potential by being shrewd businessman (i.e. savvy entrepreneurs). That, they, just like Enright, can build a flourishing life for themselves, by being true to who they are. Even if they are born poor in very difficult circumstances.

Further, Enright's life success does not just activate the values of American capitalists and American blue-collared workers. It activates the values of all Americans. Lastly, Enright's life story shows anyone— everyone really—that they too can make themselves rich, even if they were born poor. That they too can realize their personal dreams by fulfilling their selfish calling in life. For what is possible for one man to do (Enright) is possible for another man to do (you). Thus, Enright's hard-won success shows readers that economic triumph is possible for anyone, everyone really, here in America. In a free country like America. Since, in America, any person, even the poorest person, can reach a successful state-of-life. By creating-and-marketing valuable products and services in a capitalistic economy. Just like Enright does. For Enright's biography concretizes the concept that any American can get ahead in life by exercising their own unique vision. By working smart-and-hard to make their dreams come true. That they too can reach a state of spiritual fulfillment—enlightenment even—by realizing their passions. So that they, too, can be all they can be by living out who they are. For Enright's sense of rational optimism, in the face many daunting challenges, shows Americans that they too can realize their dreams by being true to their identities, even if they are born impoverished.

For Enright's life-story shows readers that only in a free country, like America, where individual rights are respected and *laissez-affair* capitalism is instituted, can a poor man like Roger Enright work his way to life-success, by providing real values in a free marketplace of goods and services. This, then, is how Enright's characterization connects with Americans in a basic way.

But Roger Enright is not the only character in the book who expresses America's founding spirit. Howard Roark also embodies American concepts of the self-made man, who rises up in life by working his own way.

To explain, like Enright, Roark is born dirt poor, in "Ohio," son of an obscure "steel puddler," with "no record of [any] relatives" to speak of (14). At age 10 he "decides to become an architect," to reshape "the earth's surface with [his] buildings," (39, 38). To learn how to build, then, Roark works many different jobs in the building trades. First, he is a rivet catcher. Second, he is a quarry worker. Third, he is a plasterer. Fourth, he is a steel-welder. Fifth, he is a plumber. And, sixth, he is an electrician. During these jobs, Roark learns how to build buildings from the ground up by shaping bolts, mining rocks, laying foundations, scaffolding buildings, fusing girders, installing pipes, and electrifying edifices. Thus, by first observing, then doing, Roark learns how to craft steel-girders that can withstand high winds. By practicing drafting he learns how to depict buildings that use the proper types of support bearing stone. By creating line drawings, he learns how to draw foundations that can support weighty stone and metal structures. By designing buildings he learns how to portray structures that can withstand strong natural forces (i.e. wind, rain, heat, and cold). By working different construction jobs

Roark learns what materials should be used in which building and why and how those materials should fit together. By being a plumber Roark learns how to picture buildings with properly laid-out pipes, apt sewage drains, fitting conduits, appropriate water ducts, and suitable sump-pumps, so that water flows into, throughout, and out of his buildings, optimally. By being an electrician Roark learns how to portray buildings with proper circuit breakers, fitting power lines, appropriate power grids, and apt electrical wires, so his buildings are adequately and efficiently electrified. In sum, by working a series of practical construction jobs early in his life, Roark not only learns how to build buildings with his hands, he also learns how to design buildings with his mind. So that his buildings can do what he built them to do.

Roark's early jobs, in turn, connects to an American sense-of-life, by showing readers that to become good in their chosen line-of-work, able Americans must not only work hard in their chosen profession to master their trade. But that they must first master one skill, at work, then learn another skill, at work, then another, then the next, and so on and so forth, until they know how to do mostly everything related to their careers. Almost anything connected to their jobs. Until they become indispensable employment assets who are highly valued by their coworkers and bosses because they know how to do so much.

Further, Roark's creative drive represents the American spirit of learning by doing. Of working a series of pragmatic jobs in a given field to master a specific trade. The novel does this by showing Americans that to gain the practical expertise they need to flourish in their careers they must work a series of different jobs in their line-of-work. For Roark's workplace ambitiousness shows readers that to be successful at work, Americans must not only learn the basic foundational skills required to do a simple job well. But they must master higher level abilities at work so they can complete harder and harder jobs. Tasks that build on the foundational skills they have learned earlier. So they are promotion worthy.

For Roark's many different jobs shows Americans that they too can be like Roark by always challenging themselves to excel. Instead of staying in their comfort zone by repeating what they already know how to do well. For Roark's continuous learning from his various jobs shows Americans that sometimes they must go outside of their wheel house to master new skills. So these Americans not only see how their related jobs fit together but also so they get a wholistic picture of their professions. So that ultimately these Americans create a flourishing career for themselves.

For ultra-successful people, like Roark, in any career are not narrow specialists, in their fields, who have learned how to implement one detail of their jobs. Rather, uber successful people – in any field of endeavor – become generalists, who know how to perfect a lot of sub-specialties related to their fields. Ergo, Roark's many different jobs show us this. Because by working manifold jobs Roark learns many different technical skills related to architecture. Yet, to do this, Roark never gets frustrated, on-the-job; he never becomes emotional, on-the-job; he is always disciplined, on the job; he is always focused, on the job; he always concentrates, on the job; since he is in full rational control of himself; on the job. (And, in his personal life, too). Thus, out in the field, Roark is persistently dedicated to his purpose; he is consistently motivated to achieve; since Roark sticks to the straight-and-narrow path of his own career trajectory. Regardless of any and all opposition. So he can achieve more-and-more in his field, even on his off time. Thereby rising to higher-and-higher levels of success in his career by working many different challenging jobs.

In sum, Roark's various jobs shows readers that Americans can succeed in anything they do by first training out in the field. By actually doing things. Which knowledge they can complement with formal schooling. Just like Roark does.

In sum, Roark first learns specific construction skills by working a series of pragmatic building jobs in the field. Then, after thousands of hours of on-the-job training, he applies these concrete skills to his drawings.

To explain, after Roark learns different job-site construction skills he enrolls in college, to complement his field training. To learn what he needs to know about the esthetics, the mathematics and the structural engineering behind building. However, once at university Roark finds he must create his own unique theory of building totally separate from Stanton's esthetic philosophy. Thus, he not only disregards the esthetic theories advocated by *Stanton* he also creates his own unique architectural philosophy by **extracting** from his formal schooling what he wants to know. Ergo, Roark does not spend his time giving his professors what they want. Rather, Roark develops his own esthetic ideology, which he refuses to debase for a teacher. He does this by selfishly reading, egotistically studying, and narcissistically drawing, in school, so he can complement what he has learned from and observed on various construction sites. Thus, through a process of selective theoretical book learning, which he complements with a practical application of that reading (i.e. his drawings) Roark *makes* himself a *genius*. Therefore, Roark attends *Stanton* to not only develop his own visual theory he also attends the university to practice designing his own buildings. To perfect his drafting skills. This practice he gets.

To explain, after learning how to build – hands on – by working many different construction jobs, Roark learns the architectural theory behind building. He does this by taking courses in architectural design, structural engineering, and mathematical science, at *Stanton's Architectural School*. In order to learn the esthetics, the physics, and the math behind building. And while Roark does learn sound structural engineering and mathematical principles at *Stanton*, sadly *Stanton* does not teach him how to design esthetic buildings. Since the university just copies what has been done before; instead of encouraging radical innovation.

However, rather than compromising his innovative vision by imitating historical buildings, Roark designs radical structures that shock his professors. Like when he draws modern geometric buildings that defy the "Tudor Chapel[s]" or the "French Opera house[s]" he was expected to create (10). Sadly, because some of Roark's professors threaten to resign if Roark is not expelled – like professor Peterkin, for example, his professor of design – Roark realizes that he must learn more elsewhere, instead of making himself miserable by staying at *Stanton*. Thus, Roark tells the Dean that he "can only find joy" in his work if he does it the best way possible to him (13). By his "own standards" (13). For he has "chosen the work [he] want[s] to do [in life]" and thus must find "joy in it," otherwise he will "condemn" [himself] to [a lifetime] of torture" (13). He elaborates by telling the Dean:

> I have let's say, sixty years too live. Most of that time will be spent working. I've chosen the work I want to do. If I find no joy in it, then I am only condemning myself to sixty years of torture. And I can find the joy only if I do my work in the best way possible to me. But the best is a matter of standards—and I set my own standards. I inherit nothing. I stand at the end of no tradition. I may, perhaps, stand at the beginning of one.

(13)

Here, Roark suggests that because his top value in life is his career focus—since working will be how he spends most of his time—he must first select a field he loves (architecture). Then he must bring unique values to that field, to the best of his ability, according to his own distinctive standards. But to do that he must set his own standards, according to his own value system. Thus, Roark does not follow any tradition whatsoever. Rather, he hopes to create a new one instead. So he can make himself profoundly happy in life by realizing his own vision.

Evidently, since Roark sees his own *selfish* happiness as the meaning, goal, and purpose of his life, Roark will not contort his soul, by regurgitating what his professors expect of him. For Roark is sure that he knows what he wants from his career and life better than they do. Therefore, Roark refuses to limit his building style by adhering to conformist visual traditions. For Roark does not want to betray himself by rising to mediocre success in conventional terms. Rather, Roark realizes that since he has nothing further to learn from *Stanton* about building, he is really happy to be expelled from the University – relieved actually – since Roark's expulsion enables him to learn how to build from the only man who can teach him to build better. Namely, Henry Cameron, the *Father of the Modern Skyscraper*, who, like Roark, also designs unorthodox buildings that revolutionize the earth's surface.

Indeed, since Henry Cameron also sees with his own eyes by creating with his own mind he shares a spiritual affinity with Roark. For both men are creative American souls who not only envision original buildings that are totally unique but also both men are primary beings who are able to make real the buildings that they imagine. The skyscrapers that they think up. For Roark realizes that what unites him to Cameron is a mastery of modern architecture. Roark comprehends this, before he even meets Cameron, by first reading about Cameron's *Dana Building*, in magazines, then by observing this structure, live, in person. For color photographs, and live viewings, of Cameron's greatest building, activates Roark's architectural values. Because after Roark looks at Cameron's *Dana* building he realizes that only a man who can build such a building can teach him what he wants to learn. Since only such a man has the vision, the skills, and the knowledge to tutor him further. For the look of Cameron's buildings, supplemented by interviews he gives about them, not only reinforces what Roark already knows about modern architecture but also shows Roark that he can learn from this great man. Because even though Roark is a young, architectural prodigy—a *wunderkind* of the highest order—he still needs to learn how to build better. He still needs to be trained by a man to improve his buildings. Since only Cameron has the architectural knowhow required to teach Roark more. This, then, is why Roark travels to *New York* to work with Cameron. So he can learn further from him.

In Cameron's office, then, Roark learns how to lay proper "foundations" without needless "stairways [and] furnace rooms;" he learns to *not* "indent [his] plans" unnecessarily; he learns how to design "country residence[s]" aptly, and he learns how to build bank buildings, expertly. (38, 38, 52). Roark learns these skills by taking directions from Cameron. By redesigning his buildings according to Cameron's instructions. For Roark refines Cameron's "sketch of a country residence" with drawings of his own (52). So that Cameron's discovery draft is "good enough to build" (52). Evidently, Roark would rather modify a country *dacha* for Cameron to improve his drafting skills; then have his designs dismissed (or rubber-stamped) by a lesser architect, who cannot appreciate, or enhance his designs. Therefore, when Cameron tells

Roark that he will "show [him] what [he] wants [done] tomorrow," since Cameron now understands "what [Roark] can do," Roark is extremely happy (56). Because Cameron is willing to train Roark. To teach Roark. So Roark can learn further. Obviously, if Cameron did not see Roark's real potential, backed by concrete skills, he would not have invested his time to teach him. But he does, which Roark appreciates. Further, by telling Roark that his initial design for the country house is "all very well" and good, Cameron encourages Roark to keep at it, since *sometimes* good designing, comes after redesigning, especially if such redesigning is steered by a grand master architect, such as Henry Cameron (56). In brief, by praising the good elements of Roark's ranch, where he can, while also showing him how to improve his *hacienda*, where he must, Cameron positively reinforces Roark's abilities, instead of just harshly criticizing him. Yet, Cameron does not micromanage Roark by hovering over his shoulder—constantly projecting quibbles about fixing small details. Rather, Cameron realizes that Roark is an extremely quick study, who just needs general instructions, from time-to-time, supplemented by specific corrections, once in a while, to produce the kinds of buildings he needs Roark to design. Ergo, because Cameron makes Roark a better builder—mostly with sticks but with an occasional carrot—he eventually creates a situation where Roark can perfect his country residence. Then Cameron delegates other projects to him mostly out of curiosity. To see what Roark will create. And, once Roark has earned Cameron's complete confidence, Cameron works with Roark jointly, to complete projects that **only** the two of them, working together, under time pressures, can finish on budget. Thus, together, Cameron and Roark design a bank building to house the *Astoria Branch* of the *Security Trust Company*. Which knowledge Roark later uses to design a *Manhattan* bank.

What is important, here, in relation to how *The Fountainhead* links to Americanism, is that learning from a mentor, is a very American experience. Since many American mentees are led by competent elders, who equip younger proteges with the specific skills they need to excel in their chosen occupations. Since they have been through it all. Thus, Ayn Rand presents in *The Fountainhead* "the relationship of the novel's hero—a young student who will later become [an] architect—to the particular teacher whom he has selected and from whom he will get the proper training" in order to emphasize this point (Art of Fiction, 76). That learning from a mentor is a very American trait.

In sum, Roark's early-life experiences [5], in the form of jobs, schooling, and mentoring, links to Ayn Rand's sense of Americanism. For Roark's biography shows readers that Americans can make themselves a subject expert in a particular field – or another – by first learning the specific skills they need to excel in that line-of-work. By working many different jobs in a specific professional field. After which, Americans can supplement their job-site training by taking university classes. So teachers can teach them more about what they want to know. After which students can hone their employment skills by conducting a formal mentorship with a person who can teach them what they want to learn better.

Ultimately, Roark's work-life shows readers that he made himself happy in life by forming his purpose early on, realizing that purpose over many years, staying with that purpose, throughout his career, and by maintaining his artistic integrity, always. For Roark's can-do American spirit, founded on optimism, hope, purpose, and drive, illustrates the basic values that made America great. That made America the clear leader of the free world. For Roark is an exemplar American hero who shows us, through his quest to become a perfect architect, that the very best Americans believe in perfection, or at least perfectibility, and try their level best, to be perfect in who they are and what they do.

Moreover, Roark's characterization shows readers that though not everybody can be a genius like a Howard Roark, they can try to be. And it is this striving; it is this pursuit of a worthy goal that makes many Americans admire, look-up to, and try to be like Roark. For Roark

---

[5] "Roark's life, in essence, shows reader's that a person should find their purpose early in life (the earlier the better) develop a keen understanding of the discipline they are passionate about—through formal education, or self-teaching, or practical experience, or a combination thereof—while simultaneously developing the practical skills they need to flourish in their chosen career, through a series of pragmatic jobs in that field. Then, they should identify who can teach them more about what they want to know. And try to work with that person. If they qualify to be his, or her, understudy." (Gurgen, 378)

"represents qualities we should admire and aspire to ourselves" (Den Uyl, 34).

Another character who concretizes the idea that *the Fountainhead* is a great American novel, is Steven Mallory. A man who rises-up in life by being true to himself. By living out who he is. A man who seeks his own happiness by accomplishing his own professional dreams. Happily, Roark creates a situation where Mallory can succeed in life by doing his work his way.

To explain, with Roark's help, Mallory turns his life around, by creating sculptures that express the highest and best within man. For thanks to Roark Mallory designs a heroic figurine of Dominique looking up to the heavens. Thanks to Roark Mallory sculpts water fountains for *Monadnock Valley*. Thanks to Roark Mallory sculpts statues for Wynand's house in *Connecticut*. Since it is Roark who saves Mallory from his rat-infested, tumble-down, *Soho* hovel. Since it is Roark who brings Mallory Wynand's patronage. Since it is Roark who prompts Mallory to fashion Dominique's nude statue. Since it is Roark who teaches Steven to disregard the indifference, the scorn, and the compromising talk, of second handers, like Peter Keating, who reject Steven, over the years, one-by-one. Because they don't want to admit that Mallory's sculptures express the highest and greatest of the triumphant human spirit.

But with Roark's help Steven learns that he **does not** have to churn out *kitsch* for people to buy. Nor does he have to prostitute his outstanding talents to appease the crowds. For Roark shows Mallory, by hiring him, that if he keeps sculpting his way not only will he make money doing what he loves but eventually he will also be recognized and valued. Even if second raters initially reject his work. Even if second handers, like Peter Keating, discard Mallory's magnificent "statue" of *Industry* for his "*Cosmo Slotnick* building lobby;" since it stands "like a challenge" to social metaphysicians like him (262). Since it conveys a slap-in-the-face to all social climbers like Peter Keating is. Because it makes normal people look "smaller and sadder [and more cunning] than usual" (226). Indeed, Mallory's giant statue of *Industry* is spurned not because it is bad. But because it is too good. Since it features a sinewy man "who looks" strong enough to burst "through the steel plate of a battleship" while regular people look weak and timid by comparison (226). For second raters, like Peter Keating, resent any art work that shows them how far they have fallen. That illustrates how lacking they really are. Thus, these people reject good art work, even though they know it is good artwork, because they do not want to be upstaged.

Ergo, because Mallory's heroic sculptures are rejected by people who do not like to be reminded that they are second raters, Steven secludes himself in his rooming house, like a wounded lion retiring to his den. And, from this sorrowful man cave, Mallory spends "two years [of his life] trying to get used to the idea" that nobody really values his statues (337). Trying to get accustomed to the notion that people do not want his figurines—even though his moldings depict human beings as strong, proud creatures, with great strength of mind-and-muscle. Thus, Mallory withdraws into a self-imposed exile, engaging in mind-altering benders, where he quaffs intoxicating tipples, usually without joy. For Mallory turns to drink to alleviate his pain at rejection; to fix the hurt he feels because nobody will pay him for his exquisite talent. Yet the booze Mallory imbibes only intensifies the anxieties he wishes he could remedy. Since his drunken bouts only escalate his "lost" and dejected mind-state. Thus, in a futile effort to numb his mind to the anguish he feels, Mallory embarks on a 24-month steady drinking binge. Trying to accept the idea that he must prostitute his "magnificent talent" to make money (338).

Thus, during his 96-week alcohol spree, Mallory painfully sculpts "a small plaster plaque of a baby sprawled on its stomach, dimpled rear forward, peeking coyly over its shoulder—the kind [that] sells in cheap gift shops" (338). Such is Mallory's last-ditch, half-hearted, bid to replenish his rapidly depleting savings. So he does not perish. For Mallory cannot find a way to make money creating the statues he wants to create, even though such a way exists. And, though Mallory does not want to waste his great abilities sculpting trite objects, he feels he must because he is so poor. To make ends meet. Since he thinks he must make money in whatever way he can. Even though he wants to mold valiant sculptures celebrating the heroic in man. Statues that depict men as heroes.

But when Roark sees this horrid plaque he is "murderously angry" that corrupt members of the intelligentsia, like Ellsworth Toohey, push gushy art onto people (338). That crooked scoundrels, like Toohey, pretend that sentimentalism, sensationalism, and slickness, is what the public should want. Roark is also livid that social climbers, like Peter Keating, enrich bad artists, because they want to benefit from their connection to wealth-and-power. Further, Roark is furious that a sculptural genius considers stooping to the schemes of a power mongering artistic dictator, like Ellsworth Toohey, to make money. He is also apoplectic that social metaphysicians, like Peter Keating, reject good art, not because they think it is bad, but because they do not want to be outdone. Because they do not want to be out-classed. Because they do not want to be one-upped. Further, Roark is upset that normal people confuse good art with bad art, since they either regurgitate what Toohey merely *pretends* is good, or mimic what Keating thinks is valuable. Instead of relying on their own independent judgement to sort the wheat from the chaff. For Roark is livid that regular folks are either brainwashed by people, like Ellsworth Toohey, or are tricked by people like Peter Keating, into abandoning their independent judgment, to blindly follow the masses. To blindly follow an authority figure. That innocents, put another way, are brainwashed into accepting tawdry, excessively gaudy, sentimental artwork, as somehow valuable, worthy, and desirable. Since they are persuaded by vulgar demagogues, like Toohey, to accept bad art as good art. Because Toohey appeals to the popular, undiscriminating tastes, of the masses, with his glib speech, to persuade people to follow him. But Roark is especially upset that certain wicked members of the intellengsia act in unison to drive a sculptural genius, like Mallory, into obscurity. Since Roark is also an architectural grand genius, who has fought against such malice all his life. Not, by actively thinking about evil doers – nor by cogitating over their schemes – but simply by creating a series of unique buildings that concretizes his own original architectural philosophy. Thus, Roark becomes enraged for the first-and-last time ever, smashing Mallory's plaque to smithereens on a wall across the room. Roark shatters this sculpture since he thinks it is a "vulgar, trite, clumsy effort to hide [an awesome] talent that [can]not be hidden." (338). An object that "belong[s] in a chamber of horrors" rather than in a gift shop (338). This, in brief, is why Roark thinks that a baby's bottom poking out at you is hardly a work of high artistic worth. Not when a grandmaster sculptor, such as Mallory, can depict man at his highest, greatest, and most heroic.

This is why when Mallory asks Roark what Howard wants him to work on, Roark tells him that he "want[s] [him] to work without asking anyone what he wants [him] to work on" (399). Here, Roark wants Mallory to be who he is by molding statues his own way. So he feels neither the need to ask anyone's permission to create the sculptures he wants to create; nor the desire to follow their suggestions, either. Since noone can improve Mallory's sculptures. Because he is the best at what he does. Further, Roark's recognition of Mallory's genius, together with his rewarding of Steven's skill, reinforces Mallory's drive to "never compromise his soul" (684-685). For Roark wants Mallory to follow his own path, instead of succumbing to the collective tastes of communal people.

To make this clear, Roark knocks Mallory's chin up, to perk Steven up; to awaken him from his severe depression. So Mallory assumes the proud body posture of somebody who is self-confident. Someone who values who they are, what they can do, and will pursue their dreams, persistently and indefatigably, until total triumph. Until they win. This, then, is why Roark gives Mallory a pep talk. To show him that despite what society, and supposed experts, think about his statues, they are objectively good. During this chat, Roark tells Mallory that he must always uphold his artistic integrity of spirit and purpose, even if it is difficult to do so. Even if he is on the brink of homelessness. Because really, he is the best sculptor alive, since Steven can create "figures not of what men are, but [of] what men could be" at their highest and mightiest (337). Since Steven can illustrate "the heroic in man" by concretizing "a magnificent respect for human beings" (337). For Roark thinks that Steven is a genius sculptor who should not care what anyone else thinks about his work. Including Roark. For Roark wants Mallory to place a high value on his work regardless of what others think about it. Since Mallory is "too good" to degrade himself by caring what neophytes think about his statues (337). By concerning himself with what greenhorns, who do not understand sculpture, think about his moldings. Indeed,

Roark is utterly surprised that a monumental sculptural genius like Mallory is twisted into such a grotesque emotional pretzel by phony pretenders who know not what they are talking about. People who are unqualified to pass valid judgment about his work, since sculpture is not their field of expertise. Here, Roark suggests that Mallory should not be dejected by people who do not have a heroic esthetic philosophy. Nor should he be saddened by people who have given up their values (i.e. their souls) long ago. Accordingly, Roark asks Mallory "What is the matter with [him], kid? What have they done to [him]? Why does he want to say things like that?" (337). Then Roark assures Mallory that he did not come to his apartment because he "felt sorry for" him (337). Nor to give him a job out of pity. Nor to get free publicity. Nor to save money. Nor because "a woman [Mallory] laid" asked him to (336). But rather for the "simple, selfish, reason," that Mallory can enhance his *Stoddard Temple* by depicting man as the clean, great, proud, and strong creature that he is. For Roark wants to work with a valiant sculptor who can complement his own heroic vision of man.

Here, Mallory is stunned that Roark came to him only because he had seen his sculptures and liked them, without knowing "anything about [him] or giving a damn" (336). For Mallory is shocked that Roark wants to buy Mallory's statues *not* because Mallory is somehow useful to Roark for his contacts. *Not* because anyone told Roark that he should like Mallory's statues. But because Roark recognizes the essential goodness of Mallory's work for himself. Thus, Roark wants to hire Mallory for that reason only. Because Roark values Mallory's statues intrinsically for what they are only. Because they are good. However, despite Roark's declaration, Mallory still cannot believe that anybody could want him for him, since until then he had dealt with a variety of second raters who had ulterior motives for seeking him out. For engaging with him. Thus, when Roark comes around, Mallory is befuddled that Roark actually cares about him, since he is accustomed to people only caring about him because of who he may know, like "the Wilson's of Podunk" (335). Not because of who he is. Thus, Mallory disbelieves that Roark will *not* drop him, once he finds a more popular sculptor, connected to people with more wealth and power. Like, "Palmer, [for instance, a sculptor] who had been recommended by Mr. Huseby," a cosmetics titan who is planning a new "five-million-dollar factory." (226). Or, Valerian "Bronson," [for example] a "sculptor who [is] a friend of Mrs. Shupe, wife of the President of Cosmo" pictures (226). Here, Mallory disbelieves Roark, since Mallory was betrayed by Keating before. (Specifically, when Keating hired Bronson not him to design a statue for his *Cosmo-Slotnick* building). Thus, to overcome Mallory's suspicion that Roark will abandon him during the final hour, Roark tells Steven that he will "write [up] a contract stating that [he] will owe [Mallory] a million dollars if [he] hire[s] another sculptor or if [his] work is not used." (335). Here, Roark needs to reassure a shattered Mallory that once he hires him for the job he will not back out of the contract. That Mallory will get paid for his work, whether it is used, or not.

Evidently, Roark views Mallory as an ally in arms—a young man who can help him improve his buildings. Since Roark realizes that Mallory is a superb visual artist who shares his own heroic spirit. Thus, after seeing how wounded Mallory is over society's rejection, Roark feels "a desire to lift [Steven] in his arms and carry him to safety" (339). Since he wants to protect Mallory from the rest of the world. Because Mallory is his "comrade-in-arms [who is] hurt in battle" (339). Thus, Roark stands "at the window [of Mallory's] wretched room," comparing Mallory's dingy domicile to a munition-pocked "shell hole" reminiscent of a "footprint of a war" (338). For Mallory's slatternly room looks like "devastation torn by [mental] explosives more vicious than any [weapons] stored in the arsenals of the world" (338). Since Mallory's crumbling tenement is not merely "an accident of poverty" (338). But the lingering battle scars of a "war against [an] enemy that [has] no name and no face" (338). Accordingly, Roark believes that Mallory's war-torn flat is the hopeless residue of a man who feels trapped between the epic forces of good-and-evil, light-and-darkness, positive-and negative. Thus, Roark analogizes Mallory's battered surroundings to what happens when a man is on the downside of an ideological struggle. For Roark sees Mallory's disgusting room as evidence of what can happen to a man who will not sacrifice his first-handed principles of beauty and truth to the second handed regurgitation of the ugly and false. Thus, to get Mallory to talk about his ideas—not about his "family, childhood, friends, or feelings," since such talk is not the main cause for Mallory's depression, but rather about "what he thinks" about life in general—Roark "pull[s] [a] chair over to [Steven's] bed" to speak to him (339). So prompted, Mallory tells Roark that though he does *not* want "to hate people," he is utterly dejected that the people around him, his supposed "best friends" even, do not love him for what really matters about him (i.e. his soul as shown by his sculptures) (339). But instead value him for less important aspects of his personality.

Further, Mallory is surprised that a total stranger actually cares "what [he] do[es,] why [he] do[es] it and what [he] thinks" since Steven is astounded that what he says is important to Roark (339). Because, up until then, Mallory has never encountered a man, in his professional, or personal, life that gave a damn about his spiritual being (i.e. the purpose, drive, and motives of his essence). Yet Mallory talks to Roark about "his work, the thoughts behind his work, [and] the thoughts that shape his life," like a "drowning man flung out to shore, getting drunk on huge, clean snatches of air." (339). Because Steven is a desperate man who is refreshed with Roark's generous receptivity to his deepest thoughts. Thus, Mallory "wish[es]," that he'd "met [Roark] before [Roark] had a job to give" him, since if he talked to Roark earlier he could have taken a better path (338). A life course free from the acerbic bitterness that plagues Mallory in waves. For if Mallory was inspired by a man like Roark earlier in his life, he would not only be the great sculptor that he is today but he would also likely enjoy his own peace-of-mind.

What is most important about all this textual analysis is that all Americans, every American, any American, wants to do their work their way. They want to take their talents, their drive, and their skills, to make money doing what they love. Thus, Mallory is ecstatic that Roark enables him to make money by doing what he loves. In a word, by being who he is. By following his own unique vision of truth, beauty, and excellence. For Roark's support of Mallory shows all Americans that when they suffer a slump, they too can find a way to turn their lives around. They too can achieve happiness, by realizing their ambitions. That what is possible for one American man to do (Mallory) is possible for another American man to do (you). This feeling, in turn, harkens to an American sense of a person making his life better by channeling the best within him. Thus, even though Mallory is introduced to readers as one of the poorest members of the novel, "a gaunt, twenty-four-year-old young man [who] live[s] [in] a dilapidated brown stone in an unlighted street that smelled of a fish market," ultimately, he turns his life around by sculpting sculptures for Roark. (334, 333).

Ergo, after gaining Mallory's willing, eager, consent to sculpt for him, Roark explains that he wants " ' Just one figure' [to] stand in' " the central courtyard of the *Stoddard Temple* (341). A statue of a naked woman who represents the best of the human spirit; (i.e.) "the heroic in man" (341). Ergo, the figure, Roark says, must be "the aspiration and the fulfillment" of absolute perfection, a figure that "seeks God, [but] finds itself" instead (341). Here, Roark asks Mallory to help him, because Mallory is the only person who can concretize through his sculptures the same spirit that Roark expresses through his buildings. Thus, now that Mallory is energized by Roark's reviving spirit, Steven becomes a new man, with a renewed sense of optimism for life. For when Steven "comes to Roark's office [the next morning] and Roark show[s] him sketches of [his Stoddard] Temple" Mallory's whole demeanor changes (340). Now there is no longer any "uncertainty in [Steven]; no remembrance of pain" (340). Instead, "when [Mallory stands] at a drafting table, with a problem to consider" he becomes completely self-assured (340). Supremely confident that he can blend his sculpture with Roark's temple—esthetically, stylistically, and spiritually—so he can amplify Roark's heroic expression. Thus, the "gesture of [Mallory's] hand taking the drawing, [is] sharp and sure, like that of a soldier on duty" who knows his job very well, since "nothing ever done to him [can] alter the function of the thing within him that [Roark] call[s] into action" (340). For Roark has brought forward and directed Mallory's creative energy, thereby giving Steven the opportunity to do what he wants with his talents and life. Ergo, because Roark has enabled Mallory to be completely who he is, Mallory has "an unyielding, impersonal confidence" when he sculpts for Roark (340). In Roark's presence. For when Mallory realizes what must be done and how to do it, Mallory becomes "Roark's equal" (340). Because when Mallory sculpts he *is* Roark's equal.

To explain, just like Roark is peerless in architecture, Mallory is matchless in sculpture, which makes both men spiritual equivalents. Worldly equals. Since both men are grandmasters of their chosen fields. Their drive, in turn, to be the best at what they do, is a very American trait.

Thus, because Roark values Mallory as America's premiere sculptural artist, he gets Mallory to wake up from his drunken stupor, by paying him to sculpt an exquisite nude statue of Dominique Francon, looking up to the stars, in a radiant pose of joy. A figurine that "immortalizes exultation; [by] emphasizing the upward glance" (Gurgen, 473). A pose that expresses Roark's own heroic life-sensations, by showing the world, via physical expression, that everything is doable, possible, achievable. That, nothing is impossible. This is why when Roark enters Steven's studio where Dominique poses for Mallory, Dominique gazes at Roark, disrobes, then "walk[s] naked to [her] stand" (345). Then, she "stand[s] straight and tense before [Mallory], throw[s] her head back, [rotates] her arms along her sides, [swivels her] palms out[wards], her body [now] alive, [with] a proud, reverent, enraptured surrender to a vision of her own" (345). Evidently, Roark activates, with his enlivening presence, Dominique's radiant inner being. So she can strike a pose that enables Mallory to express the very best within her—and, incidentally, the very best, within all human beings. Ergo, by enabling Mallory to fulfill his life's value quest, to sculpt heroic figurines, of proud men and women, envisioning grand achievements for themselves, Roark brings out Mallory's full potential. Thus, enabling Mallory to be all he can be. For Mallory is the only person on earth who can show viewers "that there is no higher reach beyond [the] form" of a sentient human organism (341). Thus, by hiring Mallory to mold Dominique's statue, Roark activates his creative American drive (i.e. his own unique genius).

Further, all this textual evidence about Mallory shows readers that Americans will help able leaders do their jobs better if those leaders give them the work they can do best. If those leaders enable them to flourish by being who they are. By doing what they are best suited to do. For Mallory, like any good American, is inspired by, and appreciative of, his leader, since with Roark Mallory becomes greater. Thus, Mallory is "very grateful [to Roark]. Not for giving [him] a job. Not for coming [to his room to save him]. Not for anything [Roark] will ever do for" him. (338). But simply for who Roark is. Since Roark's guiding example, of a supremely competent American man, with firm artistic principles, fuel's Mallory's soul with a clear moral vision. For Roark's uncompromising certainty shows Mallory that he, too, can rise to life-success, in his own way, despite many people standing in his way. By overcoming and defeating, on his own terms, any and all obstacles barring him.

Ultimately, Steven realizes – when other American men help him – that he will succeed in life. That he will realize his own American greatness through the patronage of others. This, then, is why both Gail Wynand and Howard Roark finance Mallory's artistry. Since they both think that Mallory's artwork will improve their lives materially. Thus, both men show Mallory, by buying his artwork, that if he stays the course, he will eventually be rewarded in life, by other artistic geniuses, who will help him succeed.

Accordingly, Gail Wynand, a master art critic, rewards Mallory by becoming his patron. By buying "five of [Steven's] pieces [paying] more than the dealer had hoped to ask" (455). Wynand overpays Mallory not only because he values Steven's sculptures greatly but also to reward Mallory's creative American essence.

Ergo, because of Wynand's patronage Mallory outfits his art studio with exquisite "oriental rugs, jade ash trays, [and] pieces of [magnificent] sculptures from historical excavations" (469). This, ultimately, is how Mallory is "helped by the sudden fortunes of Wynand's patronage" (469).

Likewise, Roark also financially supports Mallory by "paying for Mallory's rent, and [for] most of their frequent meals together," so that Mallory can keep sculpting how he wants to sculpt (399). Since all Mallory "needs is his time, [since he can] work without clients," while Roark cannot (399). Thus, Roark buys Mallory's time, during a building trade's depression, so Mallory can be his exclusive sculptor. So Mallory can continue to work for him. Because Roark is "competing [against] the whole country [who collectively] want[s] Mallory to [conform to their standards by molding] baby plaques," while Howard does not want

Steven to do that (399). And, Roark "likes having [his] way against theirs" (399). Thus, by giving him money, Roark ensures that Mallory can sculpt how he wants to sculpt. Because by granting him funds Roark guarantees that nobody can jerk a financial string and get Steven to comply. Ergo, by paying for most of Mallory's major expenses, Roark enables Steven to create statues his own way. So Mallory does not betray his inner purpose. This, then, is how Roark keeps Mallory on retainer. So Mallory only sculpts for him when Roark wants him to. Always and forever. For Roark enables Mallory to sculpt how he needs to sculpt by taking care of the money aspect of his artistry. So Mallory can continue to be himself. So Mallory can stay what he is. Instead of losing himself by prostituting his talents for unwise others, who collectively want him to sculpt a different way.

Thus, when Mallory comes to the attention of greater geniuses, like a Howard Roark, or a Gail Wynand, they "buy the most valuable thing that can be bought—[Mallory's] time" leaving it up to Mallory to create his own sculptures his own way (399). For Wynand and Roark both recognize and reward Mallory's genius. Since it takes their penetrating insight to identify and reward his troubled talent. Because penetrating a man's deep soul, and thus appreciating his genius, *when what is inside of him is belied by a rancorous exterior,* is difficult for most men to see. But not all. Not for Wynand and Roark. Since both Wynand and Roark appreciate Mallory's inner purity, which comes out, at times, through his sculptures.

Because of this, Mallory no longer feels like an "unrecognized genius," [6] all the time. Nor does he feel like something much worse; "the genius who is recognized yet rejected" (340). Since Mallory now feels that not all "men who see [his genius, spurn it because they] *don't* want it"

---

[6] Most geniuses struggle, at first, since they challenge the whole system of conventional ideas that defines a certain field. For instance, Einstein's articles were laughed at by the scientific community because they were so revolutionary. Due to which German journals rejected his articles, one-by-one, with scoffing derision. Eventually, however, Einstein broke through the old boy network of conservative science by keeping at it. So he could bring his genius to the attention of anyone who would listen. After which he was psychologically rewarded for his exquisite talents by being published.

and cannot handle it (340). But rather that some men, like Wynand and Roark, actually embrace it. Because they want it. Because they realize that Mallory can help them. And, though, Mallory is not angry with people for not recognizing his genius, since this is understandable, he is furious with people who reject his genius, even though they do recognize it, because they are afraid of it. In other words, Mallory is **not** upset with people for not recognizing his genius. (Since they lack the ability to recognize any genius). But he is upset with people who are scared by Mallory's genius. Which, is not to be confused with regular people, who do not know what the best is. That is okay. It is excusable. But when a man does recognize the best, and rejects it, not only is he destroying himself, he is destroying the world, in the process.

In short, Mallory's life-story connects with Americanism, since Americans like to select people who can help them realize their career goals better. Individuals, who can help them do their jobs better.

The Fountainhead also links to American values by depicting skyscrapers as "a symbol of America, of human achievement and of life on earth" (Heller, 98). Since these stone, metal, and glass towers "rise as an emblem of the independent mind in action" (Heller, 148). Rise as an example of the American creative spirit in motion. For the *Fountainhead's* "skyscrapers, [represent] the shapes of *man's achievement on earth*" (Fountainhead, 346). Thus, because Ayn Rand "wanted to write [since age 10] a story glorifying the American skyscraper [as] 'a symbol of achievement,' she chose architecture as her specific critical focus, since no profession better shows 'the creative element in man' than one which combines " 'art, and science in the sense of engineering, and business.' " (Boeckmann, 134). This, then, is why Dominique and Wynand feel exulted by *New York's* sky-line. Since they marvel at the competent American spirit that created such an exquisite city of lights on a hill.

Indeed, since the *Fountainhead's* radical *New York City* represents the forward march of human civilization it is symbolized by light. By the life-giving qualities of the sun. For a clear light often "streams from the buildings into the sky, [since] the [city's] skyscrapers [stand] like shafts of sunlight [that are] washed white by distance and summer" (600, 706).

Here, readers see that the light of *New York City's* skyscrapers beams electrical energy up into the sky, thereby radiating the creative energy of *New York City's* shinning spirits on high. To the heavens. For the "stone and plaster of the city [is] a substance that soaks the light [of skyscrapers, then] throws it back" up into the upper atmosphere for all to enjoy (600). Here, credit for creating these luminescent towers, belongs to Roark, and Roark like men, who represent the great creative energy required to create these enlivening structures. Accordingly, Roark stands "against the lights of the city," since his luminous silhouette beams to other people the spirit of man the creator (566). Specifically, of American man the arch creator, who represents the distilled essence of the highest and the best within humanity. Thus, it is only fitting that "starlight [reflects off] the ice sheets [of Wynand's] roof-top garden, [casting] the illumination proper to [Dominique's] face" (560). For American women, such as Dominique Francon, also symbolizes the essence of individuals who respect, who indeed worship, the *renascent* energy of a primary creator, such as Roark (560). This is why when Dominique rides up to Roark in a freight elevator—during the book's last scene—"the sun [not only] makes lighthouses of [the skyscrapers'] peaks" but this luminous orb also "flash[es] long white rays over the city" (727). Evidently, the book's final passage[7] belongs to Roark to honor his spiritual essence. To celebrate his creation of a shimmering city that channels—that indeed reflects—the nurturing lumens of the sun. For thanks to Roark's buildings the sun's rays beam to the far reaches of the city. Hence, it is appropriate that by novel's end, "the sun fills [Dominique's] eyes, [with] only the ocean and the sky and the figure of Howard Roark" in the foreground (727). Since

---

[7]   The "closing scene of [*The Fountainhead*] expresses the [main] idea of the book—namely, individualism. For the image of Roark standing above all else facing only the vastness of the sky and ocean gives perfect visual expression to the idea of the innovative individual looking beyond what others see. [For] the innovative individual also stands alone and looks at the world from a perspective few others see. [Since] such a person is not encumbered by pre-existing institutional structures, just as 'pinnacles, crowns, and spires,' do not obscure Roark's vision in *The Fountainhead*. [Thus, *The Fountainhead's*] final scene is an image of individualism, [which shows readers that the book] *is* a quintessentially American novel." (Den Uyl, 108).

Howard Roark is a great American architect, who casts the radiant light, of his mind's eye, over the sparkling metropolis of *New York City.*

Also, as American citizens, both Dominique and Wynand worship the sublime achievements of Americans. Thus, they both agree that people "seek[ing] a sense of the sublime [should come to] *New York [City]* [to] stand on the shore of the *Hudson,* look and kneel," so they can pay reverence to the heroic spirit that created such a city (464). For Dominique and Gail both believe that *New York City* "reveals [humanity's] true dimensions to the world." (518). Ergo both of them "love the heroic creative faculty in man'" which made these towers possible (518).

Moreover, since "both [Dominque and Gail are] in love with [N.Y.C.'s] great buildings—[with Manhattan's towering] skyscrapers"—both would give their lives to protect the city (518). For both Dominique and Gail "feel that if a war came to threaten [New York City they] would throw [themselves] into space, over the city, and protect these buildings with [their] bod[ies].'" [8] (464). Evidently, both Dominique and Gail are willing to exchange their lives to protect N.Y.C., since both characters are patriotic Americans who will do anything, everything really, to protect the highest and best within them by protecting the highest and the best within America. For they both want to protect America not simply because America is their home—and it is natural to want to protect your home—but they want to defend America because America expresses their highest secular values. Ergo, Dominique and Gail both want to protect the sanctity of their minds, by protecting the sanctity of the home of their minds—*The United States of America.* For both Dominique and Gail would rather *live free* in a free nation, or *die hard* under a dictatorship. Thus, to safeguard their civil liberties, Dominique and Wynand express sentiments articulated by the United States foundational documents, such as the *Constitution,* the *Declaration of Independence,* and the *Bill of Rights.* Which together embody their drive to actualize the best within them by protecting their individual liberties.

---

[8]   Though only Wynand says that he would trade his life to protect N.Y.C. Dominique feels the same way, since she tells Wynand that she doesn't "know whether [she is] listening to [him] or to [her]self.'" (464).

Evidently, the towers of *New York City* symbolize to Dominique and Wynand the beauty and genius of their fellow Americans. People who share their inventive spirit. Citizens who do not make a "pilgrimage to some dank pesthole in a jungle to [pay] homage [before] a crumbling temple, [by laying prostrate before] a leering stone monster with a pot belly" (463). But people who seek a sense of beauty and the sublime by contemplating *New York City* from the shores of the *Hudson River*. This is why Wynand loves seeing men "stand at the foot of a skyscraper [since] it's man who made the whole incredible mass of stone and steel" (518). For Wynand feels that such structures "do not dwarf [man, but] makes him greater than [the] structure [he built by] revealing his true dimensions to the world" (518). For what Wynand and Dominique love about *New York's* buildings is the "heroic in man" expressed by his "creative faculty" (518). Thus, Wynand says that he "would give the greatest sunset in the world for one sight of *New York's* skyline," since he thinks that a man-made metropolis, such as the big apple, supersedes nature, greatly (463). By whole orders of magnitude. Since, to him, *New York City* is a resplendent sight to behold because the "thought [and] will of man" that made it possible—that "made [it] visible"—is truly awesome (463).

Conversely, Dominique and Wynand think that it is wrong for people to "feel small before nature" because man should value themselves as the masters of nature (464). Since man ultimately tamed and shaped nature—to suit his own purposes. This is why when Wynand looks at the *Atlantic Ocean*, or the *Grand Canyon*, or the *Milky Way*, he "feel[s] the greatness of man, [the] magnificent capacity that created ship[s] to conquer all that senseless space," the great ability of people to blast "tunnels" through "mountain peaks [with] dynamite," and the wonderful capacity man has to innovate "airplanes" and spaceships, to soar to the "planets." (463). Here, Dominique agrees with Wynand's respect for man by saying that she never experiences the "particular sense of sacred rapture men say they experience in contemplating nature [except when she looks at] buildings [and] skyscrapers" (463). Conversely, Wynand thinks it is wrong for individuals to feel insignificant in relation to the strong forces of nature—thunder, tornadoes, volcanoes, earthquakes, and tsunamis—since he thinks it is wrong for human beings to believe they are simply playthings buffeted to-and-frough by natural forces beyond their control. Thus, Wynand does not feel "small when [he] look[s] at the ocean, nor at the planets, nor at mountain peaks, nor at the *Grand Canyon*," because man has invented battleships to cross Oceans, he has invented submarines to withstand waves and currents, he has invented helicopters to fly to the highest summits, he has engineered suspension bridges to traverse the *Grand Canyon's* widest chasms, and he **will** invent interstellar spaceships to fly around the universe (463). This is why Wynand rails against the idea of people "debasing themselves [before nature]" since he thinks it is a mistake to say you are "not so great when [you] look at [an awesome cataract] like *Niagara Falls*" (464). For Wynand thinks that man has created marvels that equal, even surpass, nature. Such as transoceanic ships, for example, supersonic airplanes, for instance, and deep-water submarines, case in point. Ergo, Wynand thinks it is a mistake to deprecate yourself before nature like "a leprous savage [who] smacks [his] lips in sheer glee [saying that his] best is dust before the brute force of an earthquake" (463, 464). Since Wynand thinks that "rub[bing] your forehead in the mud to the majesty of a hurricane [does not express] the spirit that leashed fire, [harnessed] steam, [tamed] electricity, [engineered] airplanes, [constructed] damns [and built] skyscrapers" (464). For mankind, continues Wynand, has "crossed oceans in sailing sloops, built airplanes and damns, and [constructed] skyscrapers" (464). Thus, human beings direct and control nature, not the reverse. For the act of traversing oceans (by ship) crossing mountains (by road) flying to places (by airplane) and exploring the cosmos (by rocket) suggests that Americans have historically conquered nature, not been conquered by nature. Thus, Wynand says that "when he look[s] at the ocean, [he] feel[s] the greatness of man; when [he] look[s] at the planets," he feels exulted by man; "when [he] look[s] at mountain peaks," he feels the majesty of man, for man, Wynand thinks, is a sublime creature, who has created, or will create, magnificent vessels to "conquer all that senseless space." (463). Here, Wynand suggests that all people, but especially Americans, have shown themselves to be the masters of nature through their creations, since it is precisely the human spirit that "leashed fire, [channeled] steam, [and harnessed] electricity" (464). Since intrepid people tamed nature to amplify their majesty as sovereign human beings. For Wynand thinks that it is both Americans, in actual fact, and spiritual Americans, from other countries, who have discovered how to direct the awesome forces of nature to realize their own goals. Goals that not only better themselves and their living situations, but goals that also advance the progress of human civilization, as a secondary byproduct. This, then, is why both Wynand and Dominique "would give the greatest sunset in the world for one sight of New York's skyline. Particularly, when one can't see the details. Just the shapes. The shapes and the thought that made them. For the sky over *New York* and the will of man-made visible" is the only "religion [they] need" (463, 464).

Further, Wynand needs a carnal example, in the flesh-and-blood, of man's ability to first pacify, then channel nature, to suit his own needs. Accordingly, when Roark has dinner with Wynand he likes that Roark is bathed in *New York City's* light. Because Wynand knows that Roark luminous silhouette represents the distilled essence of American achievement, which he casts through his shinning skyscrapers.

Further, when Wynand and Roark sail on Wynand's yacht, Gail links "thought[s] of the yacht's engine, [to] transatlantic cables, [to] skyscrapers," to Roark's architectural creations, to "everything man made" (631). Here, Wynand's stream of consciousness links the creative American spirit—of engineers, of technologists, and of builders—to Roark's architectural ability. To Roark's capacity to make his bold towers real. This, then, is why Wynand tells Roark that he "wanted to have [Roark] here with him" alone on his yacht (631). For Wynand needs Roark's presence to fuel his soul. So Wynand is inspired with a vision of man's greatness. For Roark's creative spirituality shows Wynand that man can create high artistry of great intellectual, moral, and spiritual worth. Here, Roark's example is also crucial in convincing Wynand to believe that man is clean, pure, proud, and good. Especially the best of us, which life-sensations he gets from Roark. Evidently, Dominique agrees with Wynand by saying that the "particular sense of sacred rapture men say they experience in contemplating nature" she has only experienced when she views "buildings [and] skyscrapers" (463). Here, Dominique's statement suggests that the American spirit that tamed electricity, created transistors, and invented computers, is doable for all people, as long as they share Roark's creative American spirit.

Perhaps, the best representative of the skyscraper as a symbol of American achievement is the *Father of the Skyscraper* himself, Mr. Henry Cameron. For Mr. Cameron originated the skyscraper, he gave shape to the skyscraper, by birthing the skyscraper into existence. Thus, the skyscraper is a spurt of Cameron's creative American genius. For "Henry Cameron [is not only] among the first to understand [that the] new miracle" of the modern skyscraper requires that tall buildings should look tall—like "arrow[s] of steel shooting upward without weight or limit"—but also because Henry Cameron is "among the first and the few [to] accept the truth that" skyscrapers represent the advancement of human civilization (34). Thus, because Cameron "give[s] skyscrapers [their elongated] form," he laments that other architects "curse [and moan and] wonder how [they can] make a twenty-story building look like an old brick mansion" (34). For Cameron regrets that antiquated architects "use every horizontal device available to" hide a skyscraper's "shame[ful] steel, to cheat" towers of their "height," to "shrink" towers "down to tradition," to "make [towers feel] small, safe and ancient" (34). Further, Cameron laments that these dinosaur designers draw "friezes and pediments" to obscure the height of a building. That they design triangular gable roofs to hide a building's height when they should build skyscrapers "in straight vertical lines, [with flat roofs that] flaunt [a tower's] steel and height" (34). For instead of building layered structures that rise begrudgingly on tiers and tiers of ponderous masonry, Henry Cameron is a prescient American architect who gives birth to the modern skyscraper (34). A visionary who ushers in a spirit of advanced progress to human civilization.

Toohey even acknowledges that *New York City* is "a sublime heroic achievement, which thousands [of men] worked on to create and millions of [people] profit by" (228). For Toohey thinks that had it not been for "the spirit of a dozen [visionaries] working here and there down the ages" *New York City* would not have been possible (288). For these archetypical creators, says Toohey, enabled humanity to create the resplendent *New York City* from the get go. In the first place. With their intrepid spirit. Since without the creative vision of these "twelve great [human] benefactors" continues Toohey, "none of this would be possible" (288). Which he emphasizes by sweeping his arms across *New York City's* silhouette. Then, Toohey resumes his speech by saying that though most competent people, who are good at what they do, are thankful for "the splendor of [the] achievement of these twelve great benefactors,"—since their progressive spirit pulled up the entire human race—other malicious people, who "can neither equal, nor keep," nor at least appreciate, these creator's "wealth of spirit," hate them with a passion. (288). Since they prefer to live in "a cave by an oozing swamp [and] rub sticks together," for fire light, instead of living in a "skyscraper [lit by] neon lights" (288). Since these nasty little people, with pint-sized souls, are reminded of "the [paltry] limits of their own creative capacities" by magnificent architects, like Cameron and Roark, who can create whole cities, if given a chance (288). For all these savage people are good for, infers Toohey, is living in some decrepit cave in the middle of nowhere "rubbing sticks together" for fire (288). Ergo, on one level, Toohey admires *New York City* as a symbol of man's creative essence. Yet, on another level, he insists that people who cannot match these creations, do not want to be reminded that they can create nothing worthy. Thus, they seek to raze all shrines, to bring worthy creations down to their own inept level. To tear greatness down to their own disgusting tastes. Since these people are the worst members of humanity—blustering anthropoids who want better people, to be as base, as degraded, and as vulgar, as they are. Phrased another way, Toohey asserts that instead of being inspired by the magnificent achievements of mankind (e.g. skyscrapers) some people "do not want the free gifts of other people's grandeur," since they do not want to be reminded of their own relative limits (288). Certainly, Peter Keating, does not want this reminder, since he thinks to himself, "My God, who are the men [who] made this," before remembering, with dejection, that "he had [pretended] to be one of them" (600). Yet, when Keating looks at the city from Roark's *Cord* office, he "has to speak the truth, because he [is] in the presence of the earth's greatest city" (600). Similarly, when

who shares the same noble spirit "that animated the founding fathers [9] of the United States" (Bernstein, 114). For Heller, like America's early presidents, is also a civil libertarian, who believes in a *classically* liberal country, where people can enjoy well-ordered political and economic freedoms. A land where people can relish their immutable individual rights as sovereign human beings. This is why Heller's speeches "defend the 'inalienable rights' of the individual" (Bernstein, 114).

For example, Heller's *Labor Union* speech, shows readers that he opposes state regulations, on principle: which he expresses thusly, "the only way we can have any law at all is to have as little of it as possible" (102). Accordingly, Heller "see[s] no ethical standard by which to measure the whole unethical conception of a State, except, in the amount of time, of thought, of money, of effort and of obedience, which society extorts from its every member" (101-102). Evidently, Heller views an aggressive

---

[9] The founding fathers of the United States, where **George Washington**, the commander of the Army, and the first president of America, **Alexander Hamilton**, the founder of the coastguard, and the Nation's first treasurer, **Thomas Jefferson**, the third president of the United States, a spokesman for democracy, who wrote the declaration of independence, and the bill of rights, **John Jay**, a key negotiator at the treaty of *Paris*, which ended the *American Revolutionary War* and recognized the independence of the United States, **Benjamin Franklin**, an American scientist, inventor, statesmen, and business man, who drafted parts of the *Constitution* and the *Declaration of Independence*, and who signed all of the nation's founding documents, **Samuel Adams**, the leader of the *Massachusetts Radicals*, a delegate to the *Continental Congress*, and a signer of the *Declaration of Independence*, **Roger Sherman**, an early American statesmen and lawyer, who signed the *Articles of Confederation*, and the United States *Constitution*, **Patrick Henry**, the first governor of *Virginia*, who animated America's fight for independence, by giving a 1775 speech to the Virginia legislature, where he famously said "Give me liberty, or give me death!", **James Monroe**, the fifth president of the United States, who was an American statesmen, lawyer, and diplomat, **John Adams**, America's first vice president and second president—a statesmen, attorney, diplomat, and writer—who was best known for his extreme political independence, brilliant mind and passionate patriotism, **Thomas Paine**, a political philosopher and writer, who published the first pamphlet to advocate American Independence, called *Common Sense* in 1776, **James Madison**, America's fourth president, who was nicknamed "the father of the constitution," since he wrote the **Federalist**, a book that basically lead to its' ratification, and **George Mason**, a staunch patriot who led the *Virginia Patriots* during the *American Revolution*, advocated Colonists rights, and originated the idea that man had certain inalienable rights.

national government as an unethical entity that extorts the life, energy, and production of its citizens by dictating to the public what they should (or should not) do with their lives. For Heller is a progressive democrat, who advocates a hands-off – freedom-loving – approach, where American citizens enjoy their civil liberties.

Heller also upholds the rights of workers to receive fair wages; work in safety; and labor for eight hours. He also believes that "men should work by voluntary consent, for a salary, or an hourly wage, not be forced to work a particular job, for the state". (Gurgen, 8). For Heller thinks that "the freedom to choose one's career is at the foundation of a free society." (102).

Just as Heller wants individuals to first define, then privately contract their work, Heller also supports the rights of employers to hire and fire who they like, within reason, for a just cause (102). Thus, Heller not only wants workers to be treated fairly he also wants employers to **not** be forced to accept the terms of mob worker rule at their factories. For Heller avers that just as "there is no conceivable law by which a man can be forced to work on any terms except those he chooses to set, there is no conceivable law forc[ing] [his] employer to accept" the decrees of an employee, or a group of employees (102). Since the "freedom to agree, or disagree, is [at] the foundation of [American] society, and the freedom to strike is a part of it" (102). Here, Heller means that just as an employee has a right to withdraw his labor if he feels exploited, an employer also has a right to fire any and all employees, and replace them with people who will work, under their firm but fair terms. For an employer, just like an employee, also has a right to just profits. Since the also have a right to the fruits of their labor. Because employers also have to provide for themselves and their loved ones. But, Heller continues, if the leader of an organization becomes a tyrant by expecting workers to labor for long hours, for little pay, under harsh working conditions, then workers have a right to strike against him. For imposing unreasonable expectations. Thus, Heller wants to "remind a certain Petronius from Hell's Kitchen, an exquisite bastard who has been rather noisy lately about telling [workers] that [their] strike represent[s] a destruction of law and order," that the right to strike is a legitimate right of American citizens (102).

Similarly, because Heller believes in a free civilization, with a natural order of rights, he upholds the rights of sovereign citizens, to exercise their organic liberties, as sovereign human beings. This is why he "helps political prisoners everywhere [speak up for their rights] because in defending their individual rights against the oppression of a dictator, Heller stands for political freedom, a form of independence" (Bernstein, 114-115). Thus, Heller spends more money than he can afford on "defend[ing] political prisoners anywhere," in a bid to support global freedom (101). Not only because it is the right thing to do but also to promote American freedom as well. For Heller's generous aid to freedom fighters who are wrongly imprisoned for speaking their minds, awakens a universal sense of justice. Here, Heller believes that individuals should **not** be penalized for living life as they see fit. For speaking out against the authorities. This, then, is why Heller believes that a peaceful protest, defined by peaceful resistance, and peaceful actions, does not constitute a violation of law and order, in anyway whatsoever. For political prisoners, to Heller, have committed no criminal actions, since "their only *wrongdoing* is their commitment to political freedom and to free speech in a dictatorship." (Bernstein, 99). For Heller believes that all political prisoners are guilty of is having the courage to stand up for their ideals, even if those principles are unpopular with, even dangerous to, an entrenched tyranny. This, then, is why Heller supports individuals who oppose: illiberal democracies; authoritarian autocracies; military dictatorships; tyrannical oligopolies; crushing oligarchies; subverting theocracies, or any other form of politically repressive – power mongering – government. This, then, is why Heller is a journalist "devoted to the destruction of all forms of compulsion, private and public, in heaven and on earth." (101).

This is also why Heller refuses to contribute one red cent to charity. Because Heller believes that donating money to people who do not deserve it harms the recipient of his charity. By fostering their financial dependence. For Heller believes that people who get something for nothing, when they do nothing, are incentivized to be lazy, since welfare doles artificially promotes their survival. Ergo, Heller "does not give to charities, because supporting non-working people encourages a form of dependence." (Bernstein, 114).

Further, because Heller "is a [patriot who] resents that people are 'forced to live together' [he] chooses [for the location of his house] a lonely, rocky stretch of shore, bestrewn with cliffs" (*Fountainhead*, 102 / Gurgen, 8). Since this secluded location gives him the privacy he desires. For Heller enjoys his own company well enough to be alone with himself when he wants that. Further, Heller orders Roark to build his private residence "three miles beyond an unfashionable little town in *Connecticut*," since this haven is a tax shelter, where his hard-earned money, is not extorted by the government, to support omnibus entitlement programs, that do not help him (118).

Further, since Heller is a man with individualistic American beliefs he supports Roark's sovereign soul, since Heller believes in American exceptionalism. Thus, Heller admires Roark's work for its ruthless consistency, since Heller is a man who trusts his own judgment. Thus, because Heller is "a consistent supporter of independence [he] is a friend and ally of Roark's." (Bernstein, 99). To explain, because Heller "responds to Roark's [individualistic] greatness when he sees it in Snyte's office, [he immediately offers] Roark [a] commission" to build his house (Ghate, 251). For the merit of Roark's design is the only credential that Heller requires. From then on Heller becomes Roark's friend and ally, since Roark is also a man with original judgment, just like him, who builds buildings his own way, since he sees reality independently. Therefore, after seeing Roark's radical sketch in Synte's office, Heller entrusts Roark to build his *Connecticut* house. Since he trusts Roark to build him a house as unique as his individual American identity. Since only Roark has the skill to design Heller the type of house he had always wanted—but that no other architect could create for him. Since all the architects who tried, erected something that encapsulated the group think of traditional design—not Heller's individual identity. Thus, because Roark views reality, independently, from a unique American perspective, Heller knows that "he had found the best friend he would ever have" (132). On this basis, Heller and Roark forge a close friendship. Since both individuals are unique American figures who will not budge one iota from their staunch artistic principles. Because both men are unique human beings with firm individual beliefs. For Roark, like Heller, brings out the best in himself by believing in, and creating, his own vision, regardless of the temptations, the solicitations, and the exhortations, offered by, spoken about, or urged onto them, by others. For "Roark is a structural artist extraordinaire, while Heller is a verbal artist manufique." (Gurgen, 13).

Further, Heller defends [10] the brilliant individual, since Heller, like Roark, is a distinct American person, who knows he is one of the best journalists, on earth, just like Roark knows he is one of the best – if not the best – architect in the world. Ergo, since Heller recognizes that he and Roark are kindred spirits he takes 5 main actions to help Roark: One, he tries to get Roark commissions; Two, he defends Roark when his *Enright Building* is criticized by Dominique; Three, he sits with Roark during his *Stoddard* and *Cortlandt* trials to show Roark that he also upholds the cause of an individual struggling against the collective; Four, he writes an article defending Roark's *Monadnock Valley Summer Resort*; Five, he writes an article that supports Wynand for defending Roark's *Cortlandt Homes*. Thus, to get Roark more work, Heller introduces him to Kiki Holcombe's architectural saloon. To get him jobs. He arranges various building projects—like Mr. Munday's replica of the *Randolph Place*, for instance, or Nathaniel Janss's office building, for example. All in a bid to get Roark employed. Heller also supports Roark in order to uplift an individualist architect with an independent soul. Similarly, Heller supports Roark during his *Stoddard Trial* by sitting with Roark, in the courtroom. Then, by talking to Roark, in private, when court adjourns.

Heller also supports Roark through his speech and writing. So he can bolster an individualistic architect who goes against the herd of other builders.

Accordingly, Heller lambasts Dominique for writing a questionable article about Roark's building. For Heller does not want her to mock

---

[10] By defending Roark Heller shows us that "It takes two to make a very great career: the man who is great, and the man—almost rarer—who is great enough to see greatness and say so" (Ghate, 512).

Roark for designing an apartment building loved by its residents. Thus, "With very forceful words, Heller denounces Dominique for her journalistic hooliganism" (292). Because he feels that Dominique needs to be reproached for "alloying the person and buildings of Howard Roark with the rest of the city's mediocre structures and small-minded architects" (Gurgen, 15). For Heller thinks Dominique prostituted any journalistic integrity she may have once had merely to amuse the crowd. Since Dominique's unjust criticism of Roark makes her a "journalistic tramp," to Heller, and "an irresponsible bitch" (292). Similarly, Heller also writes "an impassioned article" about Roark's "*Monadnock Valley*" in order to defend Roark's "genius" (Bernstein, 67). In this article, Heller expostulates "a ferocious cry of admiration and anger 'May we be damned if greatness must reach us through fraud!' " (536). This, then, is why Heller's article is not in his "usual calm tones, but [is] an outraged cry against injustice," instead (Bernstein, 67). Because he wants to rally people interested in the arts to support Roark.

In sum, because Heller wants "his readers to understand and appreciate the achievements of Roark's career" he writes articles that highlight the brilliant innovativeness of Roark's work (Bernstein, 67). Because just like Roark is an individualistic architect who opposes other building styles, Heller is an individualistic journalist, who opposes the crowd of other writers.

However, though Roark appreciates Heller's help, he does not need (or accept) it. For Roark will neither sacrifice his artistic integrity to comply with people that Heller introduces him to. Nor will he moderate his radical style, to suit other people's artistic tastes. Similarly, Roark will not diminish his structural principles, by working on mere copies, of copies, of other buildings, such as the *Randolph Place*, since Roark will not prostitute his visual ideals to build for anyone. Including Nathaniel Janss, of the *Janss-Stuart Real Estate Company*, or Joel Sutton, who owns an unnamed company. Further, Roark really does not need Heller's moral support at his various trials, since he ends up "supporting [his] supporters" (363). Yet, Roark does recognize that Heller tries to help him in his own way. Because Heller is like Roark to a degree. For Heller will also not give up who he is, nor water down his work, to please others. For short-term profits.

In brief, what is important here, in regards to Roark and Heller, is that they are both creative American men who must both do their work their own way. According to their own souls.

In conclusion, *The Fountainhead* is the great American novel because it shows readers that Americans, who live according to an inner truth or vision, make advances. It is also the great American novel since it shows people that individualism is what is essential to, and at the very core of, America. Further, since the book links America's founding principles to the idea that individuals are independent actors with the right to exist for their own sakes (not anyone else's) the novel shows readers that individualism manifests itself in independent judgment and productive work, not group think and stagnation. *The Fountainhead* is also a great book since it shows Americans that they should live for their own happiness and enjoy the fruits of their own freedom instead of living for the well-being of others. Moreover, *The Fountainhead* is the best example of American literature because it expresses to readers that their primary obligation is to themselves, not to others, since it "depicts [Americans as being] guided by their own conclusions [not being] in the grips of the opinions and attitudes of others" (Den Uyl, 90). The book is also a great American novel since it highlights "the model of trade—in which one person gives value for value to another"—as the paradigm of how individuals should interact with one another (Den Uyl, 99). Moreover, by showing readers that while joy is the result of a purpose driven life, while misery is the consequence of an aimless existence, the book gives voice to latent American values. Penultimately, *the Fountainhead* is a great American book since it shows readers that real American independence comes **not** from nonconformity a la Lois Cook but from being true to oneself. Since the novel shows Americans that some of civilization's values should be honored and enacted: according to the "benefits of rational living [and in-line with] the standard of" truth telling (Den Uyl, 38). Finally, *the Fountainhead* is *the* great American novel because it shows Americans that people should derive their "moral worth from [their] objective [personal] accomplishments [not] from the favorable opinions of others" (Den Uyl, 41). *The Fountainhead* is also a great American novel since it shows people that an individual's potential for excellence comes from their singular effort to reach perfection, or at least perfectibility, so they can realize a flawless connection between life, activity, and the independent mind.

This, then, is why "*The Fountainhead* is saturated with American experience, with the life of the American city, with the lives of American people pursing archetypically American occupations—businessman, journalist, builder of skyscrapers." (Cox, 7). Since by filling *The Fountainhead's* pages with "the language, the gestures, the social customs and [the] improvisations of Americans" Ayn Rand shows us that her book is "about the meaning and importance of the American individual" (Cox, 7, Den Uyl, 3).

Indeed, *The Fountainhead* is arguably the best statement ever made about American individualism. Because it expresses the true nature of individualism in a way never before clarified. By extoling individualistic virtues in a concise and unified manner. For *The Fountainhead* carries forward an individualist understanding of America by showing readers that thought and reason and action is an attribute of individuals and individuals alone. The novel does this by showing people that they can only gain a clear understanding of the world by exercising their individual judgment. This, then, is why Rand connects individualism to ideas about independence and fortitude, to ideas about excellence and integrity. Because, to Rand, life, is the standard of all action, while individual judgment is the basis of all value. This is why the individualism of many of Ayn Rand's characters is rooted in principles of successful living. Of living a successful state of life on earth. For their actions are portrayed as benefitting their lives somehow. This, ultimately, is why Rand thinks that life, and the values achieved in it, stem from the thoughts and actions of her individual characters. This is also why Rand's characters succeed because of their own choices, not because they adhere to the community, or some higher authority. Finally, because Rand thinks that individualism is critical to the successful development of one's character and consequently to success in human living, she features many different people taking a variety of independent actions.

Moreover, Ayn Rand's characters "represent the opportunity we all have to re-create ourselves anew according to a conception of what we should become" (Den Uyl, 45). Of how, in other words, we can creatively shape our souls to excel. So we can pursue self-knowledge as a means to knowing what we should become. So we can become great by being true to ourselves. For most individual human beings, to Rand, require creative shaping, to improve. To excel.

Further, since Rand shows readers that the United States is founded on the right principles, she comes across as very pro-American in *The Fountainhead*. For Rand looks to the essence of America to show readers that personal freedom is not just a desirable state but pivotal in achieving life enhancing values. Thus, the novel calls American civilization to its inherent, foundational, principles.

In sum, *The Fountainhead* is *the* great American novel not only because it is "the quintessential presentation of American individualism, optimism, and the promise that is America" but also because the novel shows America's greatness in a clear and compelling statement (Den Uyl, 14).

REFERENCES

Berliner, M.S. (Ed). (1995). *Letters of Ayn Rand*. New York City, New York: Penguin Books.

Biddle, C. (2020, July 29). Failure: A Secret Strategy for Success. Part 1. Philosophy For Flourishing Episode 9 [U-Tube Video File]. Retrieved from https://www.youtube.com/watch?v=JQIlk_h0S2o&t=45s

Bernstein, A. (2000). *Cliff Notes on Rand's The Fountainhead*. New York: Houghton Mifflin Harcourt.

Boeckmann, T. (1997). The Fountainhead as a Romantic Novel. From *Essays on Ayn Rand's The Fountainhead*. (pp. 119-153). Editor Robert Mayhew. Lexington Books, Lanham, Maryland: Rowman & Littlefield Publishers Inc..

Burns. J. (2009) *Goddess of the Market: Ayn Rand and the American Right*. New York: Oxford U.P.

Cox, Stephen. (2021, August 7) *The Literary Achievement of the Fountainhead*. The Atlas Society [Online Article / Blog Post] Retrieved from https://www.atlassociety.org/post/the-literary-achievement-of-the-fountainhead

Cato Institute. (2002). *The Declaration of Independence and the Constitution of the United States of America*. Washington, DC: Author.

Den-Uyl. D. (1950). *The Fountainhead An American Novel*. New York: Twayne Publishers.

The Fountainhead. (n.d.). In Wikipedia. Retrieved October 14, 2019 from http://en.wikipedia.org/wiki/The_fountainhead.

Ghate, O. (1997). The Basic Motivation of the Creators and the Masses in The Fountainhead. From *Essays on Ayn Rand's The Fountainhead*. (pp. 243-279). Editor Robert Mayhew. Lexington Books. Lanham, Maryland: Rowman & Littlefield Publishers Inc..

Gurgen, Emre (2021). *The Fountainhead Reference Guide: A to Z (Narrative Version 2nd Edition)*. Illinois: AuthorHouse.

Harriman, D. (Ed.) (1999). *Journals of Ayn Rand*. New York: Plume.

Heller, A. C. (2009). *Ayn Rand and The World She Made*. New York: Doubleday.

Mayhew, R. (Ed.) (2007). *Essays on Ayn Rand's The Fountainhead*. Lexington Books. Lanham, Maryland: Rowman & Littlefield Publishers Inc.

Ralston, R. (2007). Publishing the Fountainhead. (pp. 65-75). In Essays on Ayn Rand's the Fountainhead. Ed. Robert Mayhew. Lanham, MD: Lexington Books.

Rand, A. (2000). *The Art of Fiction*. New York: Penguin.

Rand, A. (2016). *The Fountainhead*. New York: New American Library.

Rand, A. (2005). *Ayn Rand Answers: The Best of Her Q & A*. Editor Robert Mayhew. New York: New American Library.

ESSAY 2

Roark the Lifegiver: *How Howard Brings Out the Best in Like-Minded Others*

Generally, Howard Roark inspires, indeed revitalizes, different characters, in *The Fountainhead*, by being a creative thinker, a moral ideal, an intellectual paragon, and a font of productive energy, who shapes perfection from imperfection by being a philosopher and an architect of the highest order. A builder, a visual designer, and a construction worker, of the greatest quality, who leads like spirited characters to also reach for the highest and best within them. By living out who they are, on their own terms, in their own way. By customizing a personal living solution for them which is modeled on Roark's basic essence. So that ultimately they learn, through Roark's flawless example, to be optimists, not pessimists, who create values, personal to them, just like Roark creates architectural values personal to him. Literary figures, in brief, who are also inspired to achieve worthy goals, in their own lives, similar to Roark, yet fitted to them, by doing those things they need to do for themselves.

Specifically, Roark inspires a young man to compose his own unique symphonies, by showing him that it is possible for him to bring his musical values to reality—just like Roark brought his unique architectural philosophy to reality—if he has hope, stays the course, and works hard. Similarly, Roark enthuses his apprentice architects, at the office, his able draftsmen, at their desks, and his construction workers, out in the field, by working smart-and-hard at these locations. Likewise, Roark assists his lover, Dominique Francon, to go from a malevolent view of society, and man's place in it, to a benevolent view of reality, and other human beings. Analogously, Roark spurs a corrupt journalist, named Gail Wynand, to revitalize his basic essence, by matching his outer actions to his inner values. Relatedly, Roark shows a genius sculptor, named Steven Mallory, that evil is metaphysically impotent, while goodness and perfection is the natural order of the universe. Similarly, Roark shows an able electrician, named Mike Donnigan, that the world eventually rewards outstanding builders—even if they are not valued and recognized for decades—if they abide by their own unique architectural course in life. He likewise shows a corporate middle-man, named Kent Lansing, that he can achieve his own passions in life—such as building the *Aquitania Hotel*—by fighting hard for his values over many years. Concomitantly, Roark prompts a businessman, named Roger Enright, to reach his own spiritual enlightenment, by creating worthy businesses, that bring tangible values into men's lives. And, finally, Roark inspires readers to excel in their own particular fields-of-thought, or lines-of-endeavor, by showing readers a believable example, in the flesh-and-blood, of a credible literary character, who recreates and transforms the earth by building a set of unique structures.

What makes Roark an even more believable example for actual readers to follow is because Roark's essence corresponds to a real-world woman named Ayn Rand. Who really did live, and breath, and achieve, her own dreams, in her own life, on her own terms. Even though the whole world was pitted against her. For Ayn Rand actually created, out there in existence, her own unique vision of the world, and man's role in it, by writing four novels, and eighteen philosophical works, despite strong social hostility to her advancement. Ergo, what makes readers even more likely to believe in and apply the spirit of Howard Roark to their own lives, is the fact that he represents the distilled essence of his creator Ayn Rand. Who was very real indeed.

For just like Roark overcomes the whole world in *The Fountainhead* to manifest his own building vision, Ayn Rand took on, and defeated, the entire globe, to publish her books. Despite stern resistance from communists from collectivists from socialists from intellectuals from journalists and from many different people. Who all attacked Ayn Rand by mocking her novels, rejecting her *Objectivist* philosophy, and attempting to squelch her voice. Yet she, like Roark, faced and defeated these people, by being herself, living out who she is, and working super smart-and-hard, regardless of their underhanded plots, mendacious schemes, and foul intrigues against her. Thereby, creating her own unique value system known as *Objectivism*.

For just like Roark decides at age 10 to be an architect, Rand decides at age 9 to be an author. Just like Roark is an architect all his life, Rand is an author all her life. Just like Roark is a construction worker from 10-22; then an architectural student from 19-22; then a draftsman from 22-26; then a civil engineer from 23-27; then a designer from 25-40; Rand is also a juvenile screen writer at 7; then a short story writer at 9; then a *novella* writer at 10; followed by a philosophy minor from 16-19; then a real screenwriter at 21; then a playwright from 21-24; then a novelist from 25-52; and, finally, a professional philosopher, from 56-76. Ergo, the parallel lives of Ayn Rand and Howard Roark shows readers that since people like Roark really do exist out there in the real world it is possible for *the Fountainhead's* readers to also accomplish their own dreams.

In *the Fountainhead*, then, Howard Roark inspires a young man, who bikes through the *Pennsylvania* woods, to find "joy, [and] reason," and hope, in his life (527). Since this youth needs to see, in concrete form, that a man was able to achieve an excellent creation, of his own, despite stern opposition. Regardless of the tastes of people around him. Since the teachings of his college—lessons about "social responsibility, a life of service, and self-sacrifice"—do not inspire this young man to compose a symphony (528). Rather, after graduating from college, this young man bikes the hills of the *Pennsylvania* countryside, to get away from the valueless world around him. So he can think. So he can find a reason to "live," not "die." (527). So he can find the courage to make his own musical dreams come true.

Ergo, to re-energize himself, so he can find the strength to go on, this young man sojourns alone, in nature, to reanimate himself. So his soul is made whole, not broken, neither by a hostile world, nor himself. During his countryside travels, then, the young man experiences joy from the resplendent sights of pristine nature. Since observing the earth's natural beauty makes him realize that life is not so bad. That it can be good, especially if "he [can] hear the hope and the promise" of his own being, expressed by the "voice [of] leaves, tree trunks, and rocks instead of words" (527). Especially, if he can find in nature, a reason to pursue his own values and goals in life, instead of giving up out of a sense of cynical resignation. Ergo, the young man turns to the beauty of pure nature, on a bright and sunny day, to disinfect his soul, through the sun's intense luminosity, so he can find a reason to live, not die [11]. So he can find a reason to go on. Peddling his bike up hill and down dale, then, through isolated clearings, swaying grain fields, and small streams, this young man's spirits are ultimately uplifted through sheer physical exertion. Through the act of physically exhausting himself. Since this exertion ultimately makes him happier because he gets in shape. Also, the azure blue skies, the babbling brooks, and the sun's solar radiance, refuels this young man's soul. Since he draws strength from nature on a picture-perfect day. But what really cheers him up is the creation of a person named Howard Roark. Whose *Summer Resort* shows him what "is possible" in life (528) [12]

Happily, after seeing Roark's *Monadnock Valley* [13] in a broad valley far below him—with houses that flow perfectly from the hillside upon which they are built—in a natural organic unity—as if nature had shaped them—the young man cultivates the intellectual vitality that

[11] By biking through the *Pennsylvania* woods, the young man girds his own being instead of ending his own life. He fortifies his own essence, instead of extinguishing his own identity. He uplifts his own soul instead of crushing his own *ethos*. He finds his own greatness, instead of caving to hopelessness. So he becomes mentally inspired, not cognitively resigned. So he becomes physically strong, not anatomically weak. So he becomes emotionally refueled, not spiritually drained. So he advances his life, instead of diminishing his existence. So he realizes his best self, instead of buckling to the world's moral grayness. So he fortifies his own vitality by being who he is, instead of giving up on himself by betraying his own dreams. So that ultimately, he has the courage to live out his own professional calling in life, instead of becoming what others what him to be.

[12] Here, the young man should follow the great *Slick Rick's* advice when he says: "Get ahead and accomplish things and you'll see the wonder and the joy life brings."

[13] Evidently, Roark's *Monadnock Valley*, shows him what is possible, doable, and achievable for him. In his own life. So that he is emboldened to strive for and accomplish his own unique dreams in music, just like Roark is emboldened to achieve his own unique dreams in architecture.

he needs to achieve his own life-enhancing values. Both, in the literal sense, of growing his physical vitality, and in the figurative sense, of leading a healthy mental and emotional life. For seeing Roark's *Summer Resort* gives this young man the courage he needs to pursue his own life's purpose by creating his own musical values. Instead of suppressing, repressing, or eliminating, the best within him, by taking his own life. And, though, the resplendent sight of plain fieldstone edifices, glistening water fountains, and large sheets of glass, makes this young man feel that he is in a "dream," that this cannot be "real," Roark assures him that what he sees is real. (529). Thus, Roark's *Monadnock Valley* shows this young man "that [joy] is possible" in life; that moral creation is possible in this world; that practical success is doable in reality (528). Because "the knowledge" of Roark's joys and achievements "give[s] this young man the courage" to realize his own personal ambitions (528). For the young man also wants to be happy and fulfilled in his life by creating his own musical symphonies, just like Roark is cheerful and content with his lifespan because he builds unique buildings during his lifecycle. Ultimately, the young man feels this way because he also wants to achieves a joyous zest for existence by following his own professional calling in this world, just like Roark is elated because he followed who he is in life to achieve success. Ergo, by observing a man who brings his own building vision into reality by being true to his own artistic integrity, the young man becomes brave enough to live out who he is, as well. Even if people disagree, agree, or are neutral, about his way of life. For seeing Roark exquisite summer resort ultimately convinces this young man that he can also bring his own greatness into reality by creating exalted music.

Roark's *Monadnock Valley* also persuades this youth that not everyone is corrupt and that not everything man-made is debauched either. That, conversely, some human beings, and their creations, are actually good, able, and worthy. Like Howard Roark, and his *Monadnock Valley* are. For the young man needs to observe a vision of human greatness by contemplating the creation and figure of a person like Howard Roark. So he can love, respect, and admire, other worthy people, by pondering "a living consciousness clean and free" (570). Instead of hating, loathing, and feeling contempt for other people, because they are second-handers. Conversely this young man learns through Roark's person that there are great people in this world, who create worthy accomplishments of their own, by pursuing their own goals, persistently and indefatigably. With firmity of purpose, surety of resolution, and staunchness of moral character. In order to achieve their own life-promoting visions. Regardless of the valueless world around them. For just like Wynand refuels his soul by contemplating the innocence of Howard Roark and his cat the young man reenergizes his *ethos* by pondering a pure vision of *Monadnock Valley* and its creator.

Concomitantly, viewing Roark's summer resort quashes this young man's *inchoate* hatred of mankind by eradicating his *incipient misanthropy*. To explain, initially, this young man "dread[s] the sight of the first house, poolroom and movie poster he would encounter" on his way back to civilization, enjoying, instead, the beauty of unsullied nature (528). He feels this way because he makes the error of mistakenly thinking that "the earth only look[s] [great] because he had seen no sign of men for hours" (527). Yet, because the young man does "not want to despise men; [but rather] want[s] to love and admire them" he searches for a worthy man-made creation that will dispel his growing repulsion for humanity (528). In fact, he looks so hard because the young man wants to be motivated by a universal respect for other human beings who have made themselves worthy of his affection by living out their dreams, instead of being reviled by the human race because *some* people are off-putting. Ergo, upon seeing Roark's magnificent summer resort the young man realizes "that man's work [can] be a higher step, [and an] improvement on nature, not a degradation" of the environment (528). Because after viewing the awesome sight of Roark's untouched summer resort the young man thinks that human beings can actually harmonize with and surpass the countryside by creating structures that fit with the exulted landscape. Instead of polluting mother earth with rubbish, trash, and gaudy man-made objects. Ergo, Roark's *Monadnock Valley* not only enables this young man to enjoy "the fresh wonder of an untouched world," but Roark's summer resort also empowers him to understand that "no artifice" tampers with what is natural and good

(527, 528). Since the ledges upon which Roark builds his houses do not lessen nature by disfiguring it but actually enhances nature by improving it. By evolving nature to fit the needs of comfortable human survival in a manner that synergizes with the physical landscape. This, then, is how Roark's summer resort transitions this young man's view from the belief that everything man-made is grossly disfiguring to the idea that sometimes human beings can create great buildings that actually improves nature.

Most significantly, Ayn Rand's vivid use of symbols, here, regarding "the boy [taking] the narrow path down the slope of the hill to [*Monadnock*] valley" signals the straight-and-narrow path he should take in life to realize his musical dreams (527). So he is not distracted by the blind-alley of over socialization; so he is not diverted by the branch path of constant career shifts and job changes; so he is not sidetracked by broad roads of mind-numbing underemployment that lead to nowhere; so he is not distracted by dead-end paths of chronic unemployment; so he is not preoccupied with windey paths of identity violating jobs. Because, ultimately, the young man does not want to travel down *nowhere* paths of complete stagnation. Characterized by no productive work, whatsoever, no creative efforts, at all, no orienting life-purpose, of any kind. Rather, he wants to make money, on his own terms, by earning revenue from his creative symphonies. By enjoying a musical life he has made for himself. Instead of living an orthodox life that society tries to impose on him. For the young man wants to earn money the right way, by living out who he is, according to his basic core-essence. Instead of pursuing a salaried career, or paying jobs, or waged employment that violates who he is deep down inside. Because he wants to create his own life by being who he is. Instead of assuming a role that society tries to force on him. Ergo, Ayn Rand's superb use of symbols, here, relating this young man's aspirations, to staying on a straight-and-narrow path in life, shows readers that just as a man should drive from point-to-point as efficiently as possible—to save money, gas, and time—so too should this young man take the most efficient passageway possible to become a first-rate musical composer.

For this young man wants to achieve his one main goal in life by staying on an exact road [14], or life-course, that will get him there. Not diminish his energies by wasting time on activities unrelated to his primary aim. Ergo, after seeing Roark's *Monadnock Valley* the young man realizes that he should travel up the road of his own career trajectory. Not wander about aimlessly in life with no clear purpose, goal, and reason to animate his days. For the young man realizes that to achieve a successful state-of-life, and thus earn his own happiness, he should pursue a narrow straight-line path that coheres with who he is inside. Lest his soul gets cast out from an earthly heaven. Ergo, Ayn Rand's pathway analogy here shows this young man that he should first conceive what he wants to do with his life (music); should second develop the skills he needs to become a composer—through formal education, or self-teaching, or practical experience, or a combination thereof—should third develop the creativity he needs to become an outstanding composer, like Mozart; should fourth map-out what specific highways (books); byways (schools); and other roads; lanes; and avenues, in the form of jobs, experiences, and mentorships, he can take to realize his dreams. (Gurgen, 448). What specific work, in other words, he should conduct to reach his particular musical destination.

If we compare the straight-and-narrow path Roark took to become a successful architect to the direct path the young man **could** take to become a successful composer we get an example for this young man's own career trajectory. Based on Roark's. Because just like Roark "decide[s] to become an architect [at] ten years old," the young man decides to "write music," during his adolescent and college years (38, 528). Further, just like Roark works his way through high school, by being a rivet catcher, a quarry chiseler, a plasterer, a steel welder, a plumber, and an electrician, this young man can also learn how to write symphonies by playing instruments, by listening to music, by learning notes, by memorizing chords, by studying keys, by recording harmonies, and by transcribing

---

[14] The young man should have a singular focus in life, by only pursing one general overall goal during his lifespan. With sub-sets of smaller goals, along the way, to actualize that one primary goal. Since being a master of one thing, instead of a jack of all trades, makes a person successful, joyous, and well paid.

melodies. So that ultimately he can become a composer by working a series of different jobs in classical music.

Ergo, just like Roark's early architectural jobs teach him how to plug steel holes in girders by placing rivets in metal orifices—so he can secure steel joists together—this young man's early musical jobs can teach him how to fill musical gaps—by plugging pleasing musical elements together. Just like Roark's early architectural jobs teach him how to chip, chisel, and jackhammer the various types of stone necessary to build, this young man's early musical jobs can teach him how to shape and combine notes. So that he understands what musical symbols represent what instruments and how they can fit together. Just like Roark's early architectural jobs teach him how to create proper foundations that are solid enough to support a building's weight above, this young man's early musical jobs can teach him how to structure music. So he can learn what cords are consonant, what cords are dissonant, and thus what sets of notes belong, and do not belong, together. Just like Roark's early architectural jobs teach him how to coat, protect, and shape, the walls, ceilings, and ledges of his skyscrapers, this young man's early musical jobs can teach him how to protect the integrity of his musical compositions. So he writes symphonies that guard against disharmony. Just like Roark's early architectural jobs teach him how to scaffold buildings by putting-up dry walls to demarcate different rooms this young man's early musical jobs can teach him the various line elements of writing music. So that he writes his music legibly and well. Just like Roark's early architectural jobs teach him how to wield a torch to sauder different pieces of metal together, this young man's early musical jobs can also teach him how to wield the musical instruments of his trade. So he can learn how to play violins, violas, cellos—harps, flutes, oboes— clarinets, bassoons, trumpets—tubas, pianos, xylophones—cymbals, triangles, drums—tambourines, chimes, and castanets. Just like Roark's early architectural jobs teach him how to build buildings with his hands by whacking hammers, hitting chisels, turning screwdrivers, and sawing files, so too can this young man's early musical jobs teach him how to write a symphony with his mind by plucking strings, strumming bows, pressing buttons, and covering holes. So the young man can also learn to handle the tools of his trade. Just like Roark's early architectural jobs teach him how to picture buildings with properly laid-out pipes; apt sewage drains; fitting conduits; appropriate water ducts; and suitable sump-pumps, this young man's early musical jobs can teach him how to lay out his musical compositions succinctly. Just like Roark's early architectural jobs teach him how to portray buildings with proper circuit breakers, fitting power lines, appropriate power grids, and apt electrical wires, this young man's early musical jobs can teach him how to represent, and place, various musical symbols, in his compositions—such as accents, bars, braces, *Caesuras*, and clefs—so that ultimately he learns how to visually represent his musical compositions. Just like Roark's early architectural jobs teach him how to craft steel-girders that can withstand high winds, this young man's early musical jobs can teach him how to structure his music to avoid *cacophony* while creating euphony. So he can learn what melodies please, and displease, the ear. Just like Roark's early architectural jobs teach him how to design structures that can withstand strong natural forces—wind, rain, heat, and cold—this young man's early musical jobs can teach him the acoustics of an aural music chamber. So he can compose resonate symphonies that are pleasing to hear. Just like Roark's early architectural jobs teach him what materials should be used in which building and why and how those materials should fit together, this young man early musical jobs can teach him what different music genres, should be played in what setting, and why. So that ultimately he can synergize these genres together in a pleasing musical arrangement. For just like Roark makes himself an outstanding builder by constructing different structures on different job sites, the young man can also become an outstanding composer by playing different instruments with different orchestras in different locations. So that just like Roark learns how to fit different structures together by working basic construction jobs early in life, the young man can also gain a unified view of how music fits together, by working basic musical jobs early in life. So that just like Roark develops, through work, the skills he needs to create esthetic buildings, the young man can develop, through jobs, the skills he needs to weave harmonious music together.

For just like Roark first starts with simple construction jobs (rivet catcher) then graduates to medial construction jobs (plasterer) followed by more advanced construction jobs (electrician)—the young man can also start with basic musical jobs (instrument player) then proceed to intermediate musical jobs (music teacher) followed by advanced musical jobs (concert master, orchestrator, and conductor). So he can finally become a *composer*. Because just as Roark's early construction jobs teach him to "place bolts, mine rocks, [mold structures], scaffold buildings, fuse girders, install pipes, and electrify structures," this young man's basic musical jobs can teach him to pick-up, pass-out, and store-music, organize concerts, perform at small local musical events, play solo instrumentals for other artists, and work as a studio musician by creating soundtracks for radio, TV, and film. (Gurgen, How the Fountainhead Expresses Americanism, www.aynrandanalyzed.com). This, ultimately, is how the young man can build his creative musical skills by working. Since his jobs can teach him what *chords*, or musical pitches are pleasing to be heard simultaneously, and thus can be blended together—what *melodies*, or successive pitches, there are in a rhythm, so he can synergize those pitches into a unified cadence—what intervals, or sound differences, are harmonic and unharmonic, and can thus be integrated together, in a pleasing assembly—what the various pitches, or sound vibrations are, that produce high tones and low tones, and how those tones can be fitted together—what sound rhythms can be fused together, and what effect this will achieve—and finally, what tones, in music and vocal sound, regarding pitch, quality, and strength, can be joined together. Because just like Roark's early construction jobs teaches him what metals—aluminum, copper, brass, and steel—and what stone—granite, limestone, marble, sandstone, and slate—can be applied in what way for what purpose to achieve what effect—the young man can also learn, through his jobs, what musical compositions can be combined together, to achieve a perfect musical symphony.

Ergo, if a specific road is closed, or highly trafficked, on this young man's life's journey, then he can reroute his path, with the same destination in mind. So he gets where he needs to go more efficiently, regardless of the man-made (or self-made) obstacles placed before him.

So he answers the call of his own greatness by enacting the courage of his own convictions. Wherever they may lead. Thereby overcoming all barriers barring his way. Be they external (from other men); be they internal (from himself); or be they hurdles he encounters in nature. So that ultimately he can overcome society, or nature, or others, or all of them, to achieve his dreams.

To be up for the job, however, the young man will surely need to make certain that his vehicle (his mind) his engine (his will) and his gas (his emotions) are all able to get him where he wants to go. Because if many doors are closed to him, the young man may need to build, and go through, his own door. An opening that is far from the beaten path that most people travel on. This effort will certainly require the young man to upgrade his mind, by getting an off-road vehicle, like a Hummer, with large wheels, and a snorkel. So he is able to cross the bumpy terrain of other people's antipathy; so he is equipped to ford the deep waters of other people's resistance; so he is able to avoid the thorny brambles of personal pricks who try to tear him down. So that ultimately he can create his own path, in life, if others are closed off to him. But first he must ensure that he is up to the task, since creating his own road, though very hard, is ultimately very fulfilling, and very rewarding, if successful. Ergo, instead of just setting off, on foot, with no concrete destination in mind, with no clear way to get there, with no obvious path of travel, first the young man must devise a goal for his life. Then he must plan a route for his journey. So he has a plan for this travels, instead of just roaming about in a confused manner [15]. Because if this young man sets out on his life's journey, with no purpose to his existence, no plan for his time, and no meaningful progression for his journey, the young man may die of mental thirst; he may perish of emotional starvation; he may die from a snake bit from a twisted person like Ellsworth Toohey. Ergo, just as someone in nature could possibly die of thirst in the desert, or starve to

---

[15] The young man needs to conceive a clear end-point for his musical efforts. Because he does not want to perish, in a struggle, he does not really understand, and is ill-equipped to handle. But instead, wants to prepare himself for musical success. By doing what he needs to do to become a great philosopher of music and composer of symphonies.

death in wastelands, or be eaten by wild animals in the wilderness, or fall off a cliff in rugged terrain, or sink into loamy quicksand, or die a million different ways—especially if he sets off on foot with no map, no compass, no water, no food, and no weapons—the young man does not want to be figuratively destroyed in a moral wilderness. Rather, he wants to make his musical dreams come true by reading good books; listening to great musical composers; and by practicing on excellent musical instruments. So that ultimately he gains the musical fuel that he needs to excel. That he needs to nourish his musical brain, sustain his musical heart, and inform his musical values. So he can travel up his own unique musical path in life, by going it alone, if he has to.

Ergo, this young man is not at risk of dying an actual physical death, in the mortal sense, through thirst, or starvation, or lack of weaponry, or because of bad navigation, he is at risk of dying a figurative death. By allowing all of his values to be drained away by others. Until he dies inside the deep recesses of his mind-and-heart. To become a walking corpse, or zombie, similar to how some people are dead inside, because they have abandoned all of their own unique values. Virtues that make a person who he, or she, is. Thus, to avoid suffering a mental-and-emotional death, at the hands of a malevolent society, this young man realizes that he must first conceive his own musical dreams. That, then, he must equip himself with the musical skills that he needs to excel.

Thus, like Roark enrolls in an architectural university called *Stanton* to further learn the mathematics, the structural engineering, and the physics behind building, the young man can also enroll in a graduate musical school, like Julliard, to learn music theory, music composition, music history, and aural skills. So, he, like Roark, becomes a great musician, by extracting from his university, what he needs to know to become a great composer one day. Such as learning how to perceive sound in meaningful patterns, the development of a hearing mind and a thinking ear, as well as a deft ability to identify a variety of rhythms. So the young man can also compose his own sort of music, by creating his own kind of symphonies, in his own free time—thereby building a musical portfolio, for himself, of sheet music—just like Roark builds an architectural portfolio, for himself, of his drawings. Which the young man can then use to launch his career.

After which the young man can seek out, interview with, and work for a mentor of his own choosing, just like Roark looks for, finds, and learns more from a mentor like Henry Cameron. For the young man, like Roark, can also find and work for a *prodigy* and *virtuoso*, like a modern-day Mozart, if he learns what composer composed what symphony, for what reason, and how such a symphony aligns with his musical talents. After which, this young man can secure an interview with this composer, to convince him to hire him, based on his musical portfolio, just like Roark finds, and works for a genius mentor, named Henry Cameron, by persuading him to hire him, by showing him his design portfolio. Then, the young man, like Roark, can develop professional musical skills through this mentor, by learning how to memorize, in one hearing, a musical piece. Then play it back, and even improve it, by improvising melodies, extemporizing chords, creating new keys, inventing new harmonies, then enhancing the piece, just like Mozart did. Further, under this mentor, this young man can hone his ability to sight read, can enhance his ability to play a piece of music that he has never played before simply by reading it off of a page of written music.

Under the competent musical direction of this mentor, then, this young man will receive objective feedback on his symphonies, just like Roark's mentor, Henry Cameron, refines Roark's drawings, by showing him how to draw them better. Likewise, the correction and oversight this young man will likely receive from his mentor – in his music studio – will certainly inform his evolution as a symphony composer. So that the young man can create different perspectives and insights into his own music, based on modification and monitoring. So that ultimately, this young man develops and grows as a musician by being trained by a musical mentor. Just like Roark learns how to design country residences, bank buildings and other structures from Henry Cameron, the father of the modern skyscraper (38). So that ultimately the young man learns transferable crossover building skills from his mentor, which he later applies to his musical compositions. For the young man can grow as an artist by applying musical lessons he has learned from his mentor to his own symphonies.

Yet just like Cameron only enhances Roark's core drawings by teaching him how to visualize his buildings more clearly—instead of defining his "aim," or end-goal, for him, the young man also **cannot** be "taught anything at the core [of his being] at the source [or *Fountainhead*] of" his creative musical drive (68). For just like Cameron tells Roark that "no one can teach [him] anything, not at the core, [or] the source of" his creative soul, noone, not even his mentor, can make this young man a lesser copy of himself. For the symphonies the young man will create in his mentor's office will be his, not his boss's, just like Roark's creations for Cameron are Roark's not Cameron's. For all Cameron does for Roark is to "teach [him how to design] better," not conceive his designs for him (68). Similarly, all this young man's mentor can do for him is to "give [him] the means, but [not] the aim— [because] the aim's [is his] own." (68). For just like Roark "won't be a little disciple putting up anemic little things in early Jacobean or late Cameron" the young man will not mimic his mentor either (68) Because the young man's "aim [is his] own," his values are his own, his essence is his own, his soul is his own, nobody else's (68). Not his mentor's. Not his school's. Not his professor's. Not his friend's. Not his family's. Not his bosses. Nobody's. No matter who they are. No matter what power they have. No matter what money they have earned. No matter who they lead. No matter how much they command. Because just like Cameron cannot strip Roark of his artistic integrity by turning him into a lackey, the young man's mentor also cannot change who the young man is at the core of his being. By turning him into a lesser version of himself. An unthinking robot who merely repeats his mentor's own style. Rather, the young man must create his own path in music, so he can create his own symphonies in life. Just like Roark must create his own path in architecture by finding his own way to build. For Cameron acknowledges that he can only give Roark the means to achieve his goals not the aim of what he should achieve in the first place. Similarly, the young man's teachers can only enhance the young man's expression of his own musical essence, not conceive his musical goals for him. Because the young man's style-of-soul is his own, not anybody else's.

Ergo, the young man, like Roark, could also create his own symphonic philosophy, just like Roark creates his own architectural philosophy, by extracting what he needs to know, from his books, from his jobs, from his schools, from his teachers, and from his experiences. For though Roark's esthetic ideology is entirely self-created, Roark is also a beneficiary of facts he has learned about the building trades. Facts he has absorbed from books, from construction jobs, from lectures, and from his own esthetic thinking. Similarly, the young man can selectively learn the ropes of music, from his fellow musicians, from his early instructors, from his band leaders, from his graduate school professors, from his private tutors, and from himself. So that ultimately the young man puts himself in a position to compose his own symphonies. For just like Roark learns about architecture by working construction jobs as a teenager, where more experienced construction workers taught him the technical skills of building, likewise, the young man can learn the technical elements of musical composition, from others, early on. Which he can then complement by reading about musical composition, by thinking about musical arrangements, by producing his own music, by practicing his own musical inventions, and by consulting his own mind. For the young man *might* need musical books, musical lessons, music teachers, a music mentor, and practical musical jobs, to put himself in a position to compose his own unique symphonies. Thereby equipping himself with a keen ability to write creative Arias; stirring Cadenzas; rousing Concertos; inspiring Movements; passionate Sonatas; *mellifluous* Operas; ardent Opuses; and moving Chamber music. Which practical experiences will not only inform the evolution of his specific musical compositions, but will also shape his own personal development, as well.

Yet the young man will have to be selective about what jobs he takes, what university he studies at, who he learns from, just like Roark is careful about all this. For just like Roark disregards the *inferior* esthetic preachings of his design professors, like Professor Peterkin, for example, who try to get him to conform to classical architecture by assigning "Tudor Chapel[s]; French Opera house[s]; [and] Renaissance Villas," the young man might also have to disregard some of the preachings of his traditional professors (10, 9). For just like Roark creates his own kinds of drawings, at *Stanton*, independent of what some of his professors want him to regurgitate, so too will the young have to compose his own kinds of symphonies, independent of what his professors may want. By using his own unique method of creation that does not merely copy what other great composers, like Mozart, Bach, and Beethoven, did classically. But instead relies on his own vision to originate new and radical classical compositions. This, then, is how this young man can form his own *sui generis* musical philosophy, just like Roark creates his own *sui generis* architectural philosophy, and just like Ayn Rand created her own *sui generis Objectivist* philosophy. So he can succeed in life in his own way, on his own terms, by creating his own symphonies. Just like Roark succeeds in life in his own way, on his own terms, by creating his own buildings; and, just like Ayn Rand succeeded in life in her own way, on her own terms, by writing four novels.

This may require him to hone his mental-and-emotional musical faculties, completely on his own, through a difficult course of self-training. Or, it may require him to apply to, and enroll in, a great musical university. In order to supplement his knowledge. Perhaps, it might be necessary for him to bypass higher-education, altogether, by seeking out, and working with, a mentor, like Mozart. So he can learn what he wants to know. Or it may require that he works several jobs in the music industry, before beginning his private practice. Or, it may require all of these things, some of these things, or none of these things. For each person's path to building a successful life for themselves is different. Thus, what Roark needed to do, and Ayn Rand needed to do, to reach their goals, may be the same, or similar, or totally different, from what the young man needs to do to make himself successful and happy in his own life.

In sum, by conceptually connecting the young man to Roark by showing readers how the former can turn out like the latter, Rand provides an idealistic, though realistic, example in literature, of the perfect man who inspires a young man to achieve his own goals in life.

Perhaps, Ayn Rand's view, that everyone, but especially young people, need to find an idealized, noble vision in life—a visualization that is realistic, not *Pollyannaish*; a depiction that is plausible, not naive—is what caused her to create a perfect man named Howard Roark. Since pondering Howard Roark is "particularly relevant to a young reader, because Roark's story is [not only] about the very struggle the young reader undergoes on a daily basis: the struggle with elders and a society that enshrines mediocrity at the expense of excellence" but most importantly it shows young people that they can ascend to greatness themselves if they persistently strive to realize their professional goals throughout their lives (Bayer). In other words, *The Fountainhead* is a principled guidepost, of the abstract philosophy of *Objectivism*, rendered through a practical sequence of believable events. For Roark succeeds, as an architect, as a lover, and as a human being, by overcoming firm resistance—at the university, at the office, with his lover, and amongst the media—by forming staunch esthetic principles. That he does not budge from at all. Not one iota. Similarly, young people, also need to believe, with convincing realism, that they too can realize their dreams, by overcoming a whole host of challenges and difficulties that they will inevitable encounter in their own careered lives. For young people, like the *Fountainhead's* young man, can also develop the strength-of-mind, the consistency-of-character, and the firm moral principles needed to create their own vision. This, then, is why the *Fountainhead* is a perennial "still-in-print" best-seller: because it is "a confirmation of the spirit of youth, [that] proclaim[s] man's glory, [by] showing [people] how much is possible" for pupils to achieve (Rand, P.). Indeed, by showing readers that the idealistic drive of youth is not a grandiose, though impractical, *naivete* that they should grow out of. But conversely, that moral action, is the only way people can achieve their own long-term lasting practical success, Ayn Rand shows readers that they can bring their own moral visions into the real world by developing a firm set of principles, just like Roark does. In brief, there are "very few [moral] guideposts to find, [in life, but] the *Fountainhead* is one of them. This is one of the cardinal reasons of *The Fountainhead's* lasting appeal: it is a confirmation of the spirit of youth, proclaiming man's glory, showing how much is possible." (Rand or Bayer).

Roark, also inspires many young draftsmen, to seek him out, to try and work for him, because they know that in his office, they will not only be recognized and valued for their own creative line drawings but, most importantly, they know that Roark will enable them to be the best they can be by being true to themselves. Since Roark is not a conventional boss, who hires people because they have embellished resumes, or because they have the right person to vouch for them, or because they have a lot of experience in the field. Rather, Roark thinks that "letters-of-recommendation," can actually be a bad thing, if those vouchers, are based on nepotism, from an industry insider, who wants to promote his family or friends, even if those family or friends are unqualified for the job (256). Similarly, Roark does not want to hire people with the wrong sort of "experience" to unlearn, since knowing how to churn out the wrong types of buildings in the wrong sorts of ways based on the wrong types of learning is not what he wants. Instead, Roark hires young draftsmen, because their "drawings," *and only their drawings*, signals to Howard that they are competent draftsmen, who qualify to work with him (256). Ergo, Roark hires youths because of what they can do; not based on who they know; or where they have worked before. Thus, Roark gives able young draftsmen *a chance* to work for him, since the buildings they can visualize, in their minds, then compose, on paper, supersedes, to Roark, who may, or may not, vouch for them (if anyone), nor what practical office jobs they have had in the past (if any) (256). For Roark realizes that to put themselves in a position to be able to draw the buildings that they can draw, these young men-and-women, these entry-level prospects, must have taught themselves; trained themselves; gained experience by themselves; by studying hard; by reading books; by practicing drafting; and, ultimately, by creating their own unique esthetic ideology which they have visualized on paper. Just like Roark does. Ergo, Roark values prospective employees based *only* on their drawings. Since their blueprints signal to him that the substance of their esthetic identity unifies with his own visual ideology, since they share his same basic "style-of-soul" (270). Thus, Roark hires potential workers only if their drawings show him that they can help him on his various architectural projects. For Roark is a transformational thinker, who only responds to the "creative capacity" of his fellow co-workers, not a transactional boss, who engages with his employees on a personal level (257). Ergo, Roark does not "smile at his employees, [does not] take them out for drinks, [does not] inquire about their families, [does not ask about] their love lives or their church attendance" (317). Since none of these factors—whether his workers are married, or not; straight, or not; attend church, or not; have a family, or not—makes them a better, or worse worker, in Roark's eyes. As long as they can do the creative job he hired them to do that is *all* that matters to Roark. For Roark believes that what his employees do on their off time, in their personal lives, in the privacy of their own homes, after office hours, is their business and their business alone. Not Roark's. This, then, is why Roark "never [speaks] to [his fellow co-workers] except of their work" (257). For Roark only:

> respond[s] to the essence of a man: to his creative capacity. [To his] competence. [For] if a man work[s] well, he needs nothing else to win his employers benevolence: it [is] granted not as a gift, but as a debt. It [is] granted, not as affection, but as recognition. [And, this meritocratic approach, which only values a person, based on their creative output] breeds an immense feeling of self-respect within every man in [Roark's] office

(317)

Evidently, Roark psychologically rewards his employees if they can create what he has hired them to create. Not only monetarily, by paying them well-earned salaries, not only intellectually, by crediting them for a job well-done, but also emotionally, by bestowing genuine goodwill on his workers because they have helped him do his job better. For Roark wants to use his time, energy, and ability, in life, to create his own buildings—not diffuse his focus, or divert his spiritual energy, by socializing with his staff, by learning about their lovers, or by understanding what *Christian* faith they have, if any. Ergo, instead of conducting courtesies typical of most bosses, Roark channels most of his mental energies into his buildings. Because he does not want to diffuse his vital life-force by cultivating smooth sets of social relationships with other people. Since

Roark cares most about other architects, who are like him, at the core level, and can help him build better.

Evidently, Roark, just like Elon Musk, inspires his employees by example. By working smarter-and-harder than anyone else, to create the buildings he needs to create. Which, in turn, inspires his workers to emulate his prodigious creative ability.

Yet it is not "loyalty to [Roark]" that makes his employees want to work so intelligently and so hard, "but [allegiance] to the best within themselves" (317). Since bringing forward, and deploying, their own productive energies to the utmost of their ability, makes Roark's helpers feel proud of what they have learned to create.

Because, like Gail Wynand, the effort Roark "demand[s] of his employees is hard to perform, while the effort he demands of himself is hard to believe," since he "pushes his employees like an army, while he pushes himself like a slave" (426). This, then, is why he often "works tire[lessly] in the office all night," which his helpers observe when they return to work "in the morning [and] find him still working" (257). Once, he even works in the office "for two days and two nights in succession," only falling "asleep on the afternoon of the third day, [for] a few hours" (257). When he awakes from these consecutive all-nighters, Roark resumes his regular architectural business as usual, by silently correcting his employee's discovery drafts (257). Without even thinking that his 48-hour working spree is unusual. For Roark is such a *Fountainhead* of creative energy that his workers soon realize that his office is not a "cold and soulless [heartless place] like a factory," as they initially thought (257). But is instead a life-giving "furnace fed" by his (and their) minds (257). For Roark has an intellectual approach that recognizes and rewards the work of the mind, not a loving approach that appreciates and remunerates the work of the heart. Yet, Roark's "staff love him," anyway, even though some of them think he is a "cold, unapproachable, inhuman boss" (316). Since Roark's cerebral method invigorates his co-workers with an electric energy that feels as if it is running through the walls of his office in energizing waves (316). And, though, they robotically apply concepts, such as "cold, unapproachable, and inhuman," to Roark because they have "been trained [to do so] by all the standards and conceptions of their past," they know, after working with Roark, that "he is none of these things" (316, 317). That he is actually the most natural, most genuine, most humane person in the world. Because, "while, at first glance, Howard Roark is a stern, austere, gloomy man, who does not laugh readily, who does not crack jokes and enjoy 'comedy-relief,' he is [actually] the truly joyous man, full of a profound, exuberant joy of living, an earnest, reverent joy, a living power, a healthy, unquenchable vitality" (Rand, Journals, 88). Because of Roark's dynamism they love Roark. Since "each man feels that, for once, he is being seen for whom he really is, for what really matters about him and for what is truly important in [his] life. [Ergo] although their friends and family say that Roark's office must be cold and inhuman, [because his workplace does not espouse accepted social values, like love, sympathy, compassion, sacrifice, and service] his employees know, without having the ability to put the knowledge into words, that for the first time in their lives they are in a *human* environment. [Thus they] experience [profound] self-respect toward themselves and loyalty and love toward Roark" (Ghate, 309). Because Roark is a personal inspiration to his co-workers by virtue of what he himself is.

Further, Roark's strong work ethic inspires his helpers (and most readers) to work hard in their own lives, as well, just like he does. Since both his coworkers, and his audience, see that working is like breathing to Roark—as natural, thoughtless, and as automatic—because he not only needs to work to sustain his life but also because he only needs to focus to create his buildings.

Thus, over-the-years, Roark labors with his mind-and-body, like a well-oiled machine. First, in high school, where he works as a common laborer—a plain workman—in the building trades. Then, "through three years" of college. Where he simultaneously works—as a "rivet catcher;" a "quarry" worker; a "plaster[er]"; a "steel" welder; "a plumber;" and "an electrician" (85, 198, 14, 211). Occasionally, he works for "fourteen hours in a row in his office, thinking he should be exhausted, but not feel[ing] so" (259). Despite this great work load, Roark loves working so hard, because he is able to produce a lot. And, because readers read this, and co-workers observe this, they are likewise inspired to achieve, those difficult jobs they know they need to do, for themselves, in their own lives.

And, though, occasionally, but not often, "Roark [makes] mistakes in choosing his employees," he lets them go when he realizes that though they *may* be qualified to work for him on a professional level, they waste time at work, on a personal one (260). Because if a young man tries to "introduce the human in preference to the intellectual," like Peter Keating, as a means to slide up the office ladder, he is fired right away, without mercy, often in less than "two weeks" (317). Since in Roark's office people are only permitted to focus on their work and careers by being substantive producers. And, conversely, are shown the door, if they try to be gamesman. If, that is, they focus some of their energies on manipulating their co-workers, instead of focusing all their time on the firm's business exclusively. Thus, in Roark's office, people who try to change the objective feel of his workplace are nixed immediately. Since Roark does not yield to psychological manipulators, like Peter Keating, who undermine the values of his office. By conniving, cajoling, and wheedling other people. Rather, Roark fires social climbers like Peter Keating from his office. For trying to change the interpersonal dynamic of his firm. Because in Roark's office people are only expected to co-operate with one another to resolve building challenges. Nothing less, nothing more, and nothing else. However, if Roark's draftsmen focus on their jobs during office hours, try hard, and are creative and honest, then Roark rewards their good work at the office. By both promoting people who create it and by retaining their employ as well. For new hires that Roark works with, "for a month," become his life-long friends (317). Because they have passed the test of Roark's critical examination, by not only performing their jobs, fairly expertly, in his presence, but also because in the office, all they do is work, because they love it.

Thus, in *The Fountainhead*, Roark has a life-giving effect on his coworkers that inspires his draftsmen, his sculptors, his electricians, and any able body, competent subordinate, who has ever worked with him, to seek him out, to work with Roark. On any, and all, of his design projects. Since his tireless energy, unquenchable vitality, and life-giving prowess, makes it an absolute joy for these men to work with Roark. Because he always knows what to do when they need his help. Since he always knows how to answer their questions. Thus, they gladly roll up their shirt sleeves and work for Roark. Either at their drafting tables, or on job sites, or hands on, or by sculpting. Even enduring deprivations to work with Roark. Since, often, Roark's former employees leave higher paid jobs in the city to work with Roark. To be guided by an able architectural leader, who knows what to do, and thus, what he is talking about. Because Roark put in the hard work, over his life, to become so knowledgeable. Which knowhow earns his men's enduring respect. Since, ultimately, Roark's workers want to be guided by him to do their jobs better. So they get better at their occupations. Ergo, money, is not what is most important to Roark's workers. Improving themselves by working with him is. Thus, their job with Roark is not drudgery, but pure joy. Because they also love what they are doing, just like Roark does. Which, incidentally, is a form of spiritual payment, that adds to hard currency payments, that they get from Roark.

This is why when Roark builds *Janer's Department Store* in *Clayton Ohio* he inspires a sense of "brotherhood" at the excavation pit of (482). Because a loyal following of construction workers are inspired by Roark's "rational discipline," at the site, because he inspires a "sense of loyalty and brotherhood" in all men there present (482, 532). By instructing his aids on how to complete construction tasks at these locations. Like when Roark points up at a rising steel frame, draws a diagram, and tells his men how to insert girders in it. When giving these instructions Roark has such a creative focus that he enthuses his coworkers with an abiding sense of loyalty and comradery for his person. For Roark always provides succinct replies to his workers queries. Because Roark has done, before, exactly what they are trying to do, now, but don't know how to do it, yet, optimally. That's fine, because Roark teaches them.

Similarly, at the *Monadnock Valley Summer Resort*, most of Roark's former draftsmen come to work for him. "Abandoning [higher paying] jobs in [*New York*] *City*" to do so (532). Despite having to live in a drafty tumble-down shanty "with wind whistling through the [dry] cracks of [the] planking;" despite having to bivouac in hastily thrown together tents on a barren hillside; despite having to work in a naked plank barrack that serves as a makeshift architectural office (532). Despite all this, all of Roark's men gladly endure physical hardships associated with this great building project. For regardless of all these challenges, Roark's men are supremely dedicated to him because he enables them to produce their best work. For working for and with Roark imbues his workers with an invigorating sense of youth, motion, purpose, and fulfillment in their souls. Since working on *Monadnock* is "the highest experience in the life of every man who [takes] part in it." (532). Indeed, Roark's employees are dedicated to building *Monadnock* because they think that the summer resort is a new beginning in their lives; a "triumphant [unstoppable] progression" that can fortify them with a clear vision of a building "achievement that nothing will stop" (532). The "wooden scaffoldings" make them feel this way (532). The "steam shovels" make them feel this way (532). The "glass rising out of the earth" makes them feel this way (532). Thus, they remember their year at *Monadnock Valley* "as the strange time when the earth stops" running and they live though "twelve months of [verdant] spring" (532).

Generally speaking, then, while Roark's workers are working on *Monadnock Valley*, they forget the trials, the tribulations, and the hassles of city life. Because while working on *Monadnock* they feel that the earth is an entirely new place where they are free to recreate nature as they see fit. Ergo, Roark's employees feel protected while they work on *Monadnock*. Not only by the steep hills and sky around them but by "the architect who walk[s] among them" (532). For Roark is the man who makes all this possible. The "thought in the mind of that man, the method of his thought, the rule of its function, stands guard over the valley and over the crusaders within it" (532).

Ergo, Steven Mallory is proud to sculpt the water fountains for *Monadnock*. Because Roark's creative excellence enables him to produce his best work.

Thus, Steven Mallory is reenergized by Roark's motivating presence. Since Roark transforms Mallory's pessimistic view of the world, and other human beings, to a gradual dawning optimism. To explain, initially, Mallory's exquisite skill, as a sculptor, is rejected by society. Not because what he sculpts is bad. But because what he molds is too good. So he retreats to his dilapidated *Greenwich Village* flat where he tries to get accustomed to the notion that his excellent sculptures are unrewarded by society because most people do not value them. And, since, Mallory is used to being ignored, passed up, criticized, or all three, he ultimately thinks that the world will not let great men, like him, survive, in their innocent pure form. Rather, he thinks that people, like Toohey, will try to corrupt him. However, instead of compromising his own soul by giving up his integrity, Mallory wallows away, for two years, partaking in intoxicating tipples, usually without joy. As an analgesic to ease the pain of his worldly rejection.

His worst fear, during his pessimistic depression, is an irrational, "drooling beast of prey," or a homicidal spiritual "maniac," that is unreceptive to reason because "some disease [has] eaten [out its'] brain" (340). A snarling, growling, monster that deploys its' cunning to destroy Mallory, instead of leaving him alone. Because the beast is not open to reason. Thus, it "can't hear [Steven] because it can't be reached, not in any way" (340). Since Steven's "eloquent words, unanswerable words," the words that make him "the vessel of the absolute truth" do not exculpate Mallory to this mindless beast (340). Not at all. Because whatever Mallory says this slobbering beast is completely unreceptive to his speech; is totally unsympathetic to his writing; is entirely unconvinced by his reasoning; and is completely closed to anything Mallory says, does, or thinks, on his behalf. For Mallory's actions do not convince this mindless beast to "not touch" him (340). Since his voice falls on deaf ears. Ergo, despite Mallory's best attempt to communicate to this beast—visually, verbally, auditorily, emotionally, and intellectually—this crazy animal, "breath[s] and move[s]" and terrorizes the defenseless Mallory in every way possible, by executing a sinister plot against him (340). Then, after the beast is done with Mallory, it ravages mankind, with a malicious purpose of its own. By prowling the earth to discover and attack weakness. Thus, Mallory's dribbling beast is responsible for world "wars" between nations, for total extermination of certain types of people, for mass genocide of different cultures, for "whole fields of butchered bodies" at root (535). For this beast, to Mallory, is epitomized, by the person of Ellsworth Toohey. Because even though Mallory "know[s] nothing about Ellsworth

Toohey, [because] he never [saw] him before shoot[ing] [at] him," he knows that Toohey is completely evil through-and-through (353). Just from his writing. Just by "read[ing] what [Toohey] writes" (353). Because after reading Toohey's communist articles in various socialist magazines, such as *New Directions*, *New Pathways*, *New Horizons*, and *New Frontiers*, after reading, in the *Daily Banner*, Toohey's Marxist articles, such as Songs and Things, Sacrilege, and I Swim With the Current, and after reading Toohey's communist book, named *Sermons in Stone*, Mallory tries to "shoot Toohey" (354). Since Tooheys columns, articles, and books, convince Mallory that "Toohey knows everything about the beast" (354). Since his writings deny human nature by preaching the sacrifice of all to all as a form of equal misery. When, in reality, people are selfish. Thus, Mallory thinks that Toohey's collectivism, will actually end in a blood bath, by promoting identical squalor for all, with Toohey as a global slave master. Since Toohey's articles, editorials, and books, which denigrates the accomplishments of competent, able, proud, builders in history—in favor of a collective race of their inferiors—makes Mallory feel that Toohey's *Marxist* philosophy of World *Communism* generates this drooling beast. Creates this tentacled hydra monster. This growling, roaring, fiend that cannot be reasoned with. Thus, to get rid of this *amorphous* beast that Toohey is responsible for hell-spawning, Mallory fires a bullet at Toohey. Since he thinks that either Toohey is this beast, or that he knows about this beast very well. Therefore, to exterminate this beast, before it grows and corrupts the world, Mallory sends a spinning bullet at Toohey's head before he "deliver[s] a [radio] address on *The Voiceless and Undefended*" (229). This, projectile, though, instead of turning Toohey's brain to goo, as intended, strikes "an inch from his face against the glass entrance of the door" to this radio station (230). Thus, dashing Mallory's hope that assassinating Toohey will quash the hideous evils that this beast will inevitably breed. Subsequently, Mallory is arrested, "on the sidewalk outside of the radio station," says nothing, on route to the police station, and is "sent to jail to await trial, [where] all efforts to question him [again] fail" (230).

Here, Mallory thinks that Toohey knows exactly why he tried to kill him. That Toohey knows that he is completely evil yet does not want the world to know it. Because he does not want to be stopped. And, incidentally, Mallory is right. Toohey is wicked and tries to hide it. Thus, when Keating tells Toohey that Mallory shot at him because he "is an incompetent and knows it and decided to take out [his frustrations] on [Toohey] because [Toohey] is a symbol of the great and able," instead of smiling, at this compliment, as Keating expects, Toohey darts a penetrating "glance" at Keating, to discover if Keating has unwittingly stumbled on his hidden nature (234). Yet, Toohey is reassured by Keating's "gaping, bewildered face," that he knows nothing (234). Because Keating's confused facial expression, "reassures" Toohey that his secret is safe from the gaze of the public for now. For people know nothing, suspect nothing, and will do nothing, about Toohey's disguised evil, at present. Yet, because Toohey confesses, at the end of the book, that he seeks to destroy values in architecture to control architecture, that he seeks to destroy values in literature to control literature, that he seeks to destroy values in theater to control theatre, that he seeks to destroy values in journalism to destroy journalism, and that he seeks to destroy values in business to destroy business, Mallory is right in believing that Toohey is absolute evil. Because in fact he is. Since Mallory sees through Toohey benevolent pretense. By penetrating to the depths of Toohey's inner rot, instead, with his laser like mind. To discover that Toohey's ultimate aim is to enthrall mankind.

But, to bamboozle the public, into thinking he is humanity's generous benefactor, patron saint, and friendly guide, when really he wants to be the world's slave-master, Toohey veils his identity, to public inspection, by telling "waiting newsman," outside the "studio anteroom," that no he "won't press charges," that no "he had never thought of himself as important enough to warrant assassination," that no he "do[es] not want to be an accomplice in the manufacturing of martyrs" (230, 249). Since Toohey wants to hide what he really is inside by affecting an unreal pose, which supersedes any desire Toohey might have to destroy Mallory. For Toohey wants to turn this deeply serious event, into a trivial happening, so journalists do not examine Toohey too closely. Lest they discover what Toohey really is. So American patriots do not flex their muscles to destroy Toohey. Thus, Toohey tries to flip the news script on the whole situation by turning a possible negative blow to his reputation, into a definite positive gloss on his persona. So people do not speculate why Mallory tried to kill him; so people do not project plausible theories about the shooting; so people do not alert the general public that something may be wrong with Toohey. So, in brief, people do not begin to question why someone would try to harm Toohey. When he appears so kind, so benevolent, so generous, so liberal. For Toohey needs to remain undetected, until it is too late to stop him. Thus, Toohey, "appear[s], unsolicited, in Mallory's defense, [at his] assault trial pleading with the judge for leniency, [because he has] no desire to see Mallory's future and career destroyed" (249). Though, everybody, in the courtroom is moved by Toohey's "extraordinary generosity," thinking gosh what a selfless kind man he is, really Toohey is a vainglorious *megalomaniac* of the first order bent on world-wide domination. However, Toohey affects a fake posture that he is the munificent father to humanity. So people believe that he is, when really he is not. This is why Toohey declares, point blank, that he "refuse[s] to be an accomplice in the manufacturing of martyrs" (249). So he can persuade people that he uplifts humanity with high principles, when the reverse is true. For Toohey does not love, nor want to help people. Instead, he hates and wants to enslave humanity, so he can become a collectivist dictator, like Joseph Stalin. Who rises to power by strong-arm, bullying, fear tactics, which he disguises, at first, by preaching love. Here, all of Toohey's sappy posturing, disgusts Mallory, to the degree that he "listens and looks at the court's proceedings, as if he is enduring a special process of cruelty" (249). But Mallory wisely "refuses to discuss his motive," in court for shooting at Toohey (249). Because he knows that if he tells the jury why he tried to kill Toohey, they would probably lock him up, in a lunatic asylum, for criminal insanity (249). Even though Mallory is sane for trying to enact extra-judicial, vigilante justice, just like Shane is sane in Jack Schaefer's novel *Shane*. However, Mallory astutely makes "no statement" whatsoever, about his motive, by prudently being quiet (249). So he does not incriminate himself for attempted premeditated murder. Waiting, instead, for the outcome of the case. Which is a two-year suspended sense contingent on probation.

However, when Roark comes into Mallory's life, and shows him that he can defeat drooling beasts like Toohey, **not** by killing them, but by ignoring them, Steven perks up. For Roark shows Mallory that wicked men, like Toohey, cannot stop him, if he minds his own business, does his own thing, and molds his own sculptures, in his own way. This is why Roark has Mallory design Dominique's statue, Monadnock's water fountains, and other sculptures. Because they enhance his buildings. This is also why Roark "pays Mallory's rent [and] most of their frequent meals together" (399). To free-up Mallory's time. So he can work on his own independent sculptures.

Also, Roark shows Mallory, by virtue of his inspiring example, what it really means to be pure, incorruptible, and clean. What it really means to be totally unafraid of Tooheylike people who try to destroy geniuses. He does this by prompting Mallory to ponder how he succeeded in creating *Gowan's Gas Station*, despite mockery from local Bostonian residents; how he was able to create the *Heller House*, despite stern resistance from his authoritarian boss named John Erick Synte; how Roark was able to create the *Sanborn House*, despite endless complaints from *Mrs. Sanborn*; how Roark was able to survive toiling in a hellish rock-quarry, to design the *Enright House*. After "spend[ing] all night thinking about" Roark's unlikely success, Mallory realizes that Roark ultimately gets what he wants because he is "terribly innocent," with his "boyish face" (340). Because the "absolute health of [Roark's] can't conceive of disease," even though he "know[s]" diseases exists (340). Here, Roark agrees with Mallory, by saying that he sought Steven out for the "same reason that makes a man choose the cleanest food he can find" (337). Because he wants to feed his mind, with Steven's nutritious sculptures. Since Steven's statues make Roark look, feel, and function, better. For Mallory's sculptures uplifts Roark's mind and emotions by portraying the soaring heights that all human beings can reach if they try. Figures that do not depict "what men are, but what men could be, and should be" at their best (337). For Mallory's sculptures show Roark not what is "probable, [for him but] what is possible," for humankind (337). Since, to Roark, Mallory's figures illustrate "a magnificent respect for human beings, for the heroic in man." (337). Ergo, Roark assures

CRITICAL ESSAYS ON AYN RAND'S THE FOUNTAINHEAD

Mallory that he will selfishly commission sculptures from him from then on, so he can promote his own mental-and-spiritual well-being. To "seek the best, for its' own sake," so Roark can revive his soul by gazing at Steven's figurines (337). For Roark needs to contemplate a benevolent life-sensation that only Mallory's statues express. Since Roark needs high quality emotional fuel to keep him functioning at peak level in life. By fueling his soul with a supreme creative octane that will energize his entire being. And, because Roark hires Steven to sculpt for him, Mallory is no longer "afraid [of the drooling beast] anymore" even though he "know[s] that the terror exists [and the] kind of terror that it is" (340). But he is afraid of it no longer. For Roark shows Mallory by example how he can overcome the beast by disregarding it altogether.

And, though Mallory relapses occasionally—such as when he is distraught that Stoddard sues Roark for his temple; or when he is upset that Bradley hires Roark to design Monadnock only because he wants the resort to fail—Roark tranquilizes Steven. By not only telling him that he has "no right to be afraid for" him but also by telling Steven that he should "go home, and forget about Bradley" (353). Because "they'll all be suing one another now, [and] we won't be dragged in and they won't destroy Monadnock" (353, 356). This, then, is how Roark calms Mallory down when he has a full head of steam.

Most importantly, when Roark becomes rich and powerful and famous after an extremely hard struggle, Mallory is happy. Glad that the A.G.A. periodical refers to Roark "as a great but unruly talent" (536). "Glad [that] the *Museum of the Future* [hangs] photographs of [Roark's] *Monadnock* [*Valley,*] his *Enright House,* [his] *Cord Building,* [and his] *Aquitania* [hotel], under beautiful glass" (536). Glad that Roark rises above various obstacles barring his way to make it on his own. For Roark's ultimate success shows Mallory what is possible for him too.

In fact, Mallory thinks that Roark has "achieved immortality," not in the literal sense that he won't die someday (470). Because he will. But in the figurative sense that Roark does not change at all at the core of his being. Despite what people do to him. For Roark does not succumb to other people's conformist vision for him. Rather, Roark consistently retains his youthful optimism by living out who he is regardless of the consequences. Instead of abandoning his childhood dreams because other people think they are impractical. This is why Mallory tells Dominique that Roark "does not change," over time, as some others do (470). That, unlike most others, who slowly die on the inside by undermining their motivating values, Roark does not "deny" himself by suppressing his properly selfish goals in life; nor does Roark "contradict" himself by doubting who he is and thus what brings him joy in this world (470). Rather, Mallory thinks that Roark realizes who he is, during childhood, then acts consistently throughout his career, because he accepts his core essence, always and forever. And, thus, does not bury his architectural values, for anyone or anything, during his time on earth. This, then, is why Mallory "can imagine [Roark] existing forever" in a this worldly sense (469, 470). For Roark's spirit, to Mallory, survives on within him. Since, Roark lives out his own self, always and forever, instead of chalking up the disfigurement of his soul to a process of personal growth, like most people do. Therefore, Mallory "can imagine [Roark] existing forever," as the essentialized essence of a perfect being (470). Since Roark's interior being, as well as his exterior actions, are always flawlessly the same. Because they always match up perfectly.

Roark, also inspires an able electrician, named *Sean Xavier Donnigan*, with a vision of tenacious resilience. Since Roark beats *almost* everyone aligned against him by living out who he is. To explain, Roark first meets *Mike Donnigan*, when Roark is an on-site engineer for Guy Francon. While conducting field inspections, Roark interacts with a master electrician named *Mike Donnigan*, who at the time lays power lines for Francon's building. The two men immediately become friends. After Roark shows him that he can walk on narrow planks thousands of feet in the sky like a facile cat walker; after Roark shows him that he can wield an acetylene expertly; after Roark tells him that he also worked for Henry Cameron. Here, Roark's revelations and demonstrations earns Donnigan's clear respect. Because both men are alike. This is why they have drinks together. During their drinking session, Roark tells Donnigan that he was fired by Francon for opposing his plans to build the *Frink National Bank Building* in a classical style. At this news, Mike gnashes his teeth, bears his incisors, and snarls a whole host of imprecations, like the bulldog that he is. Further, because he is enraged that Francon fired his best architect at the drop of a hat, for no apparent reason, Donnigan swears "savagely" that Francon is a "bastard" who is an utter moron for firing his greatest employee (90). Flabbergasted that Francon nixes his best architect arbitrarily, Donnigan wonders what Roark will do now? After learning that Roark intends to work for some other architect "of the same kind, until the same thing happens again" Donnigan wonders whether the big boys will ever let Roark succeed in his own way (90). Whether they will ever let him work on his own terms? Despite understanding that Roark will work for mediocre architects out of necessity, because wants to remain in the building trades, *Donnigan* fails to realize, at this early stage, that nobody can stop Roark. No matter how much money or power they have. No matter what they do. Because Roark is an epic genius, who is a superlative architect. First without peer. Nobody, is even close. But *Donnigan* does not know that yet. But he will. And he does. In time. Which Donnigan begins to realize when he learns that Roark forms his own private practice after working for *John Erik Synte* for 5 months. Since this job leads to Roark's first serious client, *Austen Heller*, who writes him a $500 check so he can open his own private office. Because only Roark, not *Synte*, can design Heller's dream home how he wants it. Here, Donnigan begins to see that Roark eventually gets his way. Regardless of any opposition pitted against him.

Upon this discovery, Donnigan decides to surprise Roark, by working on his *Heller House*. To not only show Roark that he morally supports him but also because *Donnigan* enjoys working with Roark. Since Roark creates jobs that *Donnigan* is proud to be a part of. Thus, when Roark arrives at the job and spots Mike's "husky figure enmeshed in electric wires" he is astounded that Mike left his usual bigger jobs— like a job he was working on at the time in *Philadelphia*—for "such a come-down" (130). When before Mike never "bother[ed] with small private residences" (130). In response, Mike insists that he would not miss Roark's "first house" for the world (130). That working for Roark it is not a come-down but actually a come-up. Since it is an honor for Donnigan to work for Roark. Since Roark is so able a builder, so great a teacher, and so wonderful a person that Mike will "not [willingly] miss

his office, when the time is right, or "someone will send for [him] before then" (198). Insisting that he won't "give the sons of bitches the kind of treat," of getting Roark a job in a "construction gang, here, in town,"—because it saddens Donnigan's to see Roark performing like a side "show freak for all the bastards in New York to see,"—so they can gloat that they "brought [Roark] down like that"—Donnigan arranges for Roark to get a job in "a granite quarry down in *Connecticut*" (198). Donnigan gets Roark this job because he has "worked for that bastard Francon's pet contractors for so long," that he has turned the "foreman" of his granite quarry into "a great pal of [his]" (198). Grateful, Roark consoles Mike that everything "will be all right," (198). That Donnigan should not feel sorry for him, since Roark does not feel sorry for himself. Because he'll be back, before long, even stronger than before. Here, Roark's insistence that Mike should not care what other people think about Roark, prompts Mike to say "Okay, Red," (198).

However, Mike is still gloomy about Roark's career in architecture because he disbelieves that Roark can come back from the rock quarry. Despite what Roark tells him. But after Roark returns from the granite quarry to build a radical apartment building for Roger Enright, Mike is astonished. He is shocked that Roark can rise-up like that again, when the odds are stacked against him. However, Mike realizes, after witnessing Roark's astounding come-back, that though the "granite quarry [made him] very sick once, turn[s] out it made no difference at all, in the long run' " (358). Since Roark just goes on building buildings his own way, according to his own unique architectural philosophy, regardless of any, and all, hurdles blocking his ascent. This is why Roark builds the *Aquitania Hotel*, the *Cord Building, Janer's Department Store*, and *Monadnock Valley*, exactly as he wants to. Facing down any and all opposition to do so. Which ultimately prompts Donnigan to tell Mallory "not to worry, [because Roark] can't lose, quarries or no quarries, trials or no trials, [since] they can't beat him, Steve, they just can't, not the whole goddamn world" (532).

Evidently, Roark's unstoppable drive makes Donnigan believe that all of architecture's phony pretenders will be permanently put in their place by him. That all of the "office boys, [who can't] do a man's work," will be outsmarted by a lowly construction worker (84). That all of the "college smarties," with advanced degrees, will be bested by a man who dropped out of University. That all of "the teacher's pets sent down from [Francon's] office," will be outhustled by a genius builder who does not conform (84, 85). Therefore, he is refreshed, when a genius architect, named Howard Roark, rolls up his shirt sleeves, and gets busy, doing an honest day's work on building sites. Since Roark is Donnigan's kind of construction worker—a builder who upstages lesser architects aligned against him by building his own way regardless of their best efforts to suppress him. For Donnigan loves that Roark sticks it to Guy Francon, to Peter Keating, to John Erick Synte, to Gus Webb, to Ellsworth Toohey, to Ralston Holcombe, to all the lesser architects he is used to dealing with. Since Roark's triumph over these builders shows Donnigan that eventually, grand geniuses, like Roark, will ascend to the pinnacle of their own greatness, by doing their own thing. Regardless of who does not like it.

Similarly, Roark inspires a corporate middle-man named Kent Lansing to build "a luxurious hotel on *Central Park South*" regardless of the executive board's resistance to the project (319). Because after viewing Roark's *Enright House* and *Cord Building*, Lansing seeks Roark out to fight for his designs. Since Roark's designs coheres with Lansing's desire to get the corporation's executive board to accept the best hotel possible for the company. Ergo, after seeing Roark's *Enright House* and *Cord Building*, Lansing decides that he must hire Roark to build the *Aquitania Hotel*. Since Lansing also has business integrity as a corporate salesman, just like Roark has building integrity as a structural architect. For Lansing, like Roark, also has "certain standards of what is good," which he "stand[s]" by come hell-or-high water (321). Thus, he hires Roark to build *The Aquitania* hotel, since only Roark can "give [him] what he want[s]" (320). Because only Roark has integrity like he does. Thus, Lansing fights hard for weeks to get Roark's designs accepted by the *Aquitania's* executive board. Overcoming objections like Roark is "not a regular fellow," that he is not accepted in architectural circles, that other board members are not going to vote for him, that he is too unorthodox for personal safety (320). But Lansing overcomes the reservations of board members, like Mr. Harper, Mr. Macy, Mr. Palmer, Mrs. Pritchett, Mr. Thompson, Mr. Thorpe, and Mrs. Betsy, by showing them that they should not be afraid to deliver their own judgments. Because their independent votes will result in a good hotel being built for their corporation, even if their decision violate the field's consensus. This, then, is why Lansing battles against the board of directors of the *Aquitania Corporation*. Because to him the:

> board of directors is one or two ambitious men—and a lot of ballast. [A] vacuum, really, [comprised of a bunch of spineless cowards] or great big empty [personal] nothings, [who do not have the vision nor the guts to hire a great architect, when they see him]

(320)

Here, Roark opines that because executive boards are typically feckless "do-nothing" institutions normally he can't get along with them. Because they usually vote against him as a group. But when people are not in a group but alone, Roark thinks that they are much more reasonable. Because they exercise their own independent judgment. But when they function in groups, or committees, or boards, people become irrational. So Roark thinks. Since agreeing with a murky consensus, takes priority. Not determining what's best for a given company. This, then, is why Roark appreciates that a scrappy figure, named Kent Lansing, who loves fighting for his architectural principles, battles hard to get Roark's designs accepted. Because otherwise the *Aquitania's* executive board would not hire Roark. But they do because of Lansing.

Sadly, construction stops on *Aquitania* before the hotel is completed. Because two of its' owners go bust gambling on the "stock market," while a third owner, "get [most] of his funds attached [in a] lawsuit," over a disputed inheritance, while a fourth owner's funds are seized for "embezzle[ing] some[one] else's [Aquitania] shares" (345). And, though, the corporation that owns the *Aquitania Hotel* explodes in "a tangle of court cases" that takes years to untangle, eventually Lansing gets the new board to resume construction (345). After the court cases resolve. For Lansing vows to "straighten it out even if he has to [figuratively] murder a few" board members to get the project restarted (346). So that the *Aquitania Hotel* does not remain empty and unfinished, for years, with piles of rubble and cement around it. But is completed instead. Evertrue to his word, Lansing eventually arranges for the cement dust to be removed from the hotel; for the frame of the hotel to be rebuilt; for gaps in the hotel's windows to be plugged with cement caulking; and for the hotel to be electrified.

Indeed, Roark energizes this prize fighter, this battering ram, this submarine torpedo, this tank of a man named Kent Lansing, to get what both of them want. By giving Lansing a worthy cause to fight for. By giving Lansing a valuable project he can believe in. By giving Lansing a substantive building he can crusade for. Not simply because the *Aquitania* is a magnificent hotel in its own right. But primarily because this modernist hotel is what is best for Lansing's corporation. This, ultimately, is why Lansing crusades on Roark's behalf by ensuring that his *Aquitania Hotel* is created. Because, in the final analysis, Lansing is happy that individuals, such as Roark, enable him to advocate what is in his own best business interests. This, then, is why Lansing thinks that Roark is worthy of his persuasive efforts with the board. Since what Roark brings to the table, in his relationship with Lansing, is an all-encompassing drive for esthetic excellence. Thus, because "Lansing is a salesman with a rare appreciation of artistic genius and an even rarer willingness to fight for it" he is happy to promote an architect who is worthy of his help (Bernstein, Cliff's Notes).

In sum, what is most important about all this analysis of Roark, Lansing, and the *Aquitania* hotel, is that Roark and Lansing do not quit building the Aquitania because they meet stern resistance. Instead, they build the hotel in their own way. Until they win total victory with the board.

Similarly, Roark also adds to and enhances the entrepreneurial energy of an astute businessman named *Roger Enright* by enabling him to create the *Enright House* and the *Cortlandt Project*. So that Enright adds two additional pioneering businesses to his portfolio of five other successful businesses. For thanks to Roark, Enright is not just the proud owner of an oil business, a restaurant, a radio shop, an auto-garage, and a refrigerator plant, he expands into the real estate market, as well. Becoming a commercial property owner in addition to a raw energy producer, a food maker, a transistor manufacturer, an automobile fixer, and an appliance manufacturer. Who fulfills himself spiritually by finding an architect who can create the radical structures that he needs built. So he can earn even more money.

To explain, Roger Enright is a serial entrepreneur, who is always looking for viable opportunities to expand into other business sectors. His new vision is to design an apartment complex that is different from any other housing unit in *New York City*. Though he has the money to finance the project, he does not have the creative vision, to originate the building idea. So he searches for an architect for six months to build him a radical apartment building that will revolutionize modern housing for the residents of *New York City*. For six months, then, he looks for an architect who has the creative vision, the technical expertise, and the building knowhow to deliver him the kind of revolutionary apartment building that he wants. But the average architects that he interviews do not have the unconventional daring necessary to give Enright what he wants. So he composes a distinctive "newspaper advertisement for his unique apartments [that functions] like a personal invitation to Roark: the kind of chance created expressly for him" (256). Unable, to get an interview with Roger Enright himself, Roark is interviewed by Enright's secretary, who dismisses Roark's designs because Roark lacks the experience he is looking for. For Enright's secretary is a conventional conformist who has already made up his mind about Roark in advance. Thus, he thinks "that Mr. Enright would not be interested" in Roark, because Roark was expelled, fired, and is a pariah with other architects (256). This, then, is why Enright's secretary looks infinitely bored during his interview with Roark. Since he has already rejected Roark in advance. Ergo, he only speaks with Roark, out of a sense of perfunctory *pro forma* courtesy. To give him the impression that he is entertaining all options; even though he does not. Rather, Enright's secretary dismisses Roark, ahead of time, without even giving him a chance to shine, because he has prejudged him unfit to build.

However, because Enright has seen Roark's revolutionary buildings, he tries to discover if Mr. Roark is the right architect for him. By recalling him from a rock quarry in *Connecticut* to his offices in *Manhattan*. After a half hour interview, then, Enright hires Roark right away. Since Enright knows that Roark has the ability to deliver him what he wants. Which is a "new type of apartment building, with each unit complete and isolated like an expensive private home." (174). A magnificent "apartment building that [does not] look like anything anywhere else." (174). This, then, is how Enright overcomes his initial architectural frustrations by finding Roark.

Yet, because Enright's secretary is an orthodox mediocrity, who simply judges Roark on paper, instead of making the effort to realize what he can do—not just who he knows, or what office experiences he has—he laughs Roark out of his office. Yet because of this gross negligence, Enright fires his secretary, without a moment's pause, for overlooking Roark's exquisite building skills. For Enright cannot have a stupidly conservative secretary working for him. An incompetent subordinate who simply goes through the motions of his employment search. Instead of taking the time, and making the effort, to contemplate all options, even if they do not seem viable at first. Thus, because of his secretary's callous oversight, Enright discharges his secretary in the "middle of a busy day," ordering him to leave "a half-typed letter" in his typewriter (256). So he can exit the building in "ten minutes" (256). With a security escort to usher him out safely. That's what Enright's secretary gets for lacking the vision to bring Roark to his boss's decision-making attention.

Thus, Enright selects Roark as his architect because he knows what he likes (when he sees it)—because he acts on what he likes (when he conceives it)—and because he goes with what he likes, immediately. Without a moment's hesitation. Ergo, after Roark shows Enright his plans for the *Enright House*, Roger orders Roark to "proceed with construction at once" (256). Because Roger trusts his methodical business instincts to lead him on the right money-making path. For Enright is a hard-nosed individualist, whose business acumen usually coins him money.

To make sure he will make money with Roark, though, Roger occasionally monitors the progress of the *Enright House*. To ensure that he was right to choose Roark. This is why Enright inspects the excavation pit of the Enright House. So he can ask Roark questions like "How's it going?" and "Do you have everything you need?" (293). Happily, Roark replies that "yes" he has everything he needs for the job, which is "two days ahead of schedule" (293). After Roark explains to Enright "the layout of future rooms, the system of elevators, the heating plant, [and] the arrangement of windows, they [stand together] talking about the job, like brothers" (293). Bonded by the seal of radical competence. Elated by Roark's friendship, *Enright* is proud to reveal the *Enright House*, with Roark, to a few friends, weeks ahead of schedule, in June of 1929. And, though Enright "frowns fiercely, [at this informal soft opening] as if he [is] about to scream with rage, his friends, [including Howard Roark] know that Enright [is] happy" (315). Because they know that Enright is a perfectionist, just like Steve Jobs was, because Enright must also ensure that every detail of his building is perfect before the formal reveal. In sum, because Enright makes choices that are best for him and his companies, based on observable facts, verifiable data, and clear statistics, he is delighted to have enlisted Roark's prodigious talents to deliver him a successful rental unit.

After making money with Roark on the *Enright House*, Roger re-hires Roark to design *Cortlandt Homes*. So he can earn more profits. To realize this aim, Enright first "buys the site, the plans and the ruins of Cortlandt from the government" (719). Then he prepares the excavation pit for Roark, by "order[ing] every twisted remnant of the foundations, [to be] dug out [and transported away] so Roark has a clean hole in the earth, to work with." (719). Then he "hire[s] Roark to rebuild the project, [who, in turn, hires] a single contractor to observe the strict economy of [Roark's original] plans (719).

Evidently, *Enright* selects Roark to be his builder again because only Roark can deliver a housing project to Enright that costs little to build and less to rent. Because Enright wants to "set low rentals with a comfortable profit margin for himself" (719). Thus, to ensure this fair, but firm, rate of return, Enright directs his rental agent to **only** rent to people if they have the money to pay a reasonable rent. Not because they are needy indigents; or have a low income; or are struggling workers; or have several mouths to feed; or because they have a meagre diet. But because they can pay rent themselves, without relying on tax payers to foot the bill. For Enright, through Roark, converts this former "bleeding-heart" governmental housing project into a for-profit private economic enterprise that is "open to anyone who wishes to move in and [can afford to] pay the rent (719). Whether "they have the financial means to afford a more expensive apartment elsewhere, or not" (719). For Enright, like Roark, believes that it is unjust, through public taxation, to "penalize a man because he earns forty dollars a week," in favor of a man who makes only fifteen (604). For both Enright and Roark believe that a diligent earner, who works hard, to make a better life for himself, should not have to pay unjust governmental taxes to finance a government housing project, that actually drains his own money away, while simultaneously disqualifying him from renting in that project, because he makes too much money. This double injustice, then, is unconscionable to both Enright and Roark, because it penalizes the middle and upper classes, in favor of the indigent lower classes. Since it punishes hard working earners, who are usually rich, in favor of lazy loafers, who are usually poor. These shared values, in turn, further cements the bonds of Enright and Roark's energizing friendship.

Similarly, Howard Roark also revitalizes a corrupt publisher named Gail Wynand by showing him that first-handers—like Roark is and like Wynand could have been—can flourish in this world. By being themselves. By authentically connecting to who they are, deep down inside, so they can fully achieve and maintain a strong connection to their ideal or real selves. In all contexts, and in all situations. Both on the inside and on the outside.

To explain, initially, Wynand meets Roark since he is looking for a builder to design a country home for Dominique Wynand, his newlywed wife. Because Wynand has seen and likes Roark's buildings, he wants to meet Roark to see if he should hire him. Thus, when Wynand meets Roark he not only discovers that Roark can deliver to Wynand the private home that he wants but he also learns that he loves Roark. Because he recognizes that unlike him, Roark succeeded in his own way, on his own terms, by being true to himself. Wynand admires this because instead of being a first-hander like Roark is, who has his own architectural values, Wynand is a second-rater, whose media empire does not reflect his true-self. Yet, because he wants to shed his perverted exterior shell to embrace his health-giving inner essence, Wynand loves Roark. Because Roark shows him how to connect with, and emphasize, his best self. So that he can be a first hander just like Roark is by reconnecting to his inner greatness. Thus, thanks to Roark's life-giving influence, Wynand is able to realize his best self.

Ergo, thanks to Roark's stimulating inspiration, Wynand fires Dwight Carson. So this young man can resume his natural calling in life to be an individualist writer. Moreover, thanks to Roark's benevolent guidance, Wynand quashes excessively disgusting stories in the *Banner*. So that his newspaper no longer peddles totally outrageous stories, like it usually does. Additionally, thanks to Roark's enlivening presence, he defends Roark in the court of public opinion, by advocating clean stories that are "a gracious tribute to the greatness of [Roarks] artistry" (617). Stories that do not feature "Roark at breakfast" (617). But stories that are only "a considered, gracious tribute to the greatness of his [visual] artistry" (617). Furthermore, thanks to Roark's positive sway, Wynand writes wholesome articles – for a change – free of the *Banner's* usual sensationalism. Articles that undercut the usual populist smut that Wynand features in his *Daily Banner*. Moreover, thanks to Roark, Wynand "kills three of [Scarret's grossest stories] when "before he never did that" (547). Telling Scarret to "go easy on the bilge [because] there is a limit even for intellectual depravity' " (547). This, then, is how Roark prompts Wynand to kill lurid "human interest" stories; bogus sentimental crusades; filthy anti-rich articles; garish demogic photographs; and mob-mongering writings, before they see the light of day. For Roark's presence is enough to dissuade this media mogul from circulating this written filth in the first place.

Thus, after befriending Roark, and dating Dominique, Wynand feels "thirty years younger" (422). Because Roark's life-giving influence causes Wynand to reconnect with his pure inner essence. Causes Wynand to rediscover his best self. Which he does by projecting the idealistic hope that he had when he was young. A time in his life when he still had honest values in his soul. Such as his youthful drive to defend an honest police captain named *Captain Mulligan*, who was being framed by a corrupt political machine. But Wynand cannot stand this because "Pat Mulligan, [who is] police captain of his [local] precinct, [was] the only honest man he had ever met in his life" (422). Ergo, after Wynand meets Roark, spends time with Roark, and is bested by Roark, he feels very happy, since he thinks, for the first time, that life is really quite easy and joyous. Therefore, Wynand feels carefree, he feels foot-loose and fancy-free, he feels light as a bird, he feels thirty years younger, after he spends time with Roark. Since Roark enthuses Wynand with a benevolent sense-of-life. That anything is possible, doable, achievable, since Roark did what he wanted to do with his life, despite heavy social opposition.

Thus, Roark restores to Gail, by virtue of his living example, the highest and most noble qualities that Gail merited as a youth. His integrity, his morality, his optimism, and his hope. Which confidence, ultimately prompts Wynand to align himself with Roark. Because Wynand knows that Roark is there to help him. That Roark has such confidence in Wynand's inner purity that he tries to spur Wynand to save his own soul. Before it is too late.

Ultimately, Roark's resounding success inspires Wynand to become a better man. Since Roark's achievements show him that *real* success is possible for first-handers. Accordingly, Roark prompts Wynand to transcend his vice-ridden outer self to embrace his health-giving inner being. Thereby, modeling his soul on Roark's example. Thus, by drawing energy from Roark's revitalizing essence, Wynand suggests that he too may evolve to Roark's level in time. If he tries hard enough. For Wynand believes that what one man can do another can do, especially if two men are alike in many intrinsic ways despite having extrinsic differences. Accordingly, Wynand needs to be with Roark so he can learn from Roark. So he can fuel his mind, evolve his emotions, and purify his essence, with Roark's counterbalancing example. This is why Wynand frees Roark, defends Roark, feeds Roark, cruises with Roark, and visits Roark. So he has the necessary exposure to be like Roark.

Roark also reenergizes Dominque by getting her to fully accept his *Objectivist* philosophy. Not by forcing it on her, but by showing it to her, through his person. To explain, initially, Dominique has a pessimistic philosophy, which holds that human beings cannot reach greatness, try as they may, because an inimical society, bent on their destruction, will inevitably block their paths to excellence. That, conversely, only unprincipled gamesmen—people who flatter, who connive, who cajole, and who deceive—can succeed in the game-of-life. By always being what others want them to be instead of being themselves. Yet when Roark succeeds in life by being who he is and by creating his own architectural values Dominique discards her nihilistic ideology altogether in order to embrace his *Objectivist* Philosophy.

To explain, because Dominique has witnessed, in her life, secondhanders, like her father, Guy Francon, his protégé, Peter Keating, and her husband, Gail Wynand, manipulate other people to become rich and famous, she believes that only people who form fake social bonds with others can succeed in life. Evidently, Dominique feels this way because she has observed her papa, his disciple, and her hubby, become wealthy and powerful, over time. Not because they are superior architects, like Howard Roark, or great journalists, like Austen Heller. But because they hide their lack of substance by either smooth talking them, over fine wines and gourmet meals, like Guy and Peter do. Or they disguise their hollowness by using sensationalism to rabble rouse the crowd, like Gail Wynand does. So affluent customers either accept their designs-and-commissions, thereby enriching them, or so that the general public buys their newspapers, thereby making them wealthy. And, when she sees positive scoundrels, like Toohey, succeed in life, even though he wants to enslave humanity, Dominque thinks to herself that the world deserves Toohey.

And, though, at first, Dominique thinks to herself that it is utterly impossible, for an arch genius, like Roark, to succeed by producing new buildings that transform the earth's surface, eventually her viewpoint changes. It changes when Dominique sees Roark build the *Heller House, Gowan's Gas Station, Janer's Department Store, Monadnock Valley, Wynand's Connecticut House, Cortlandt,* and sundry other buildings, despite stern opposition. It changes when she witnesses Peter Keating's tragic dissolution. It changes when she sees Roark win his *Cortlandt* court case. It changes when she sees evil men like Toohey lose their jobs. Because of these changing indicators, Dominique exchanges her former belief that the world will not let Roark move forward in a progressive direction for a new belief that the world cannot stop Roark. That the Roark's of this world can and do succeed on their own terms, in their own way, even if they are strongly resisted, for awhile, since they are creative visionaries who find a way to accomplish their goals. If they staunchly pursue their values, work extremely hard, and do not listen to anyone, but themselves, regarding their own work. This, then, is what makes Dominique change her philosophy from pessimism to *Objectivism*. Because Roark's success ultimately convinces her that his *Objectivist Philosophy* is valid.

Her worldview also changes when she sees Roark make spiritual friends, with Henry Cameron, Austen Heller, Mike Donnigan, Steven Mallory, Roger Enright, Gail Wynand, and their subordinates. Since Roark's newfound friends signals to Dominique that there are other great men out there as well who recognize and value Roark's greatness.

Dominique is especially enthused when she observes these men defend Roark because they love him. And, thus, wish to prevent his person, his ideas, and his soul, from being subjected to mocking, to ridicule, to misunderstanding, and to mistreatment, from unthinking others. For Dominique becomes happy, when she realizes that other men defend Roark because they are like Roark, on some level. And, thus, take concrete actions to prevent him from being maligned, traduced, and otherwise lampooned, by the mob. Basically, because they want to protect the best in themselves. For they need Roark in their lives. To energize, them, with his **Objectivist Architectural Philosophy.**

This, then, is how Dominique transitions from an arch pessimist who rejects Roark's philosophy, to an arch optimist who accepts Roark's philosophy.

Roark, in essence, is also a model for readers, because he realizes his dreams, regardless, of stern opposition. Since he is naturally always him, and thus, does not change his being, to please others, which is a good quality. Because it is always best to be yourself, regardless of who likes you, or not, since authentic genuiness, or realness-of-soul, or a consistent character, ultimately promotes a healthy mental and emotional life.

Further, Roark's strong work ethic, of working long hours, to realize his building passions, inspires readers—at least this one—to also work hard, in their own lives, without being terminally discouraged. Without giving up on their dreams, to pursue a lesser life. So they can also ascend to greatness, to the best of their abilities, according to their ambitions, and in line with the skills and talents they have developed thus far. So they, like Roark, can also create a good life for themselves, by actualizing their ideal, or real, selves.

Regarding how Roark's logical soul brings out the same in his readers let's analyze how Roark's childhood jobs, his university experiences, and his professional employment, ultimately leads to his final success. Since his early drive, his later persistence, and his ultimate career goals, jibes with the reader's career ambitions. By showing readers how they can also succeed in their own lives.

To explain, Roark works extremely hard, throughout his life, to attain success, on his own terms, in his own way, in one field-of-thought, in one line-of-work, just like readers should as well. This is why, as a teenager, he works many different jobs, in the building trades, so he can save enough money, for his education, while gaining the hands-on practical skills that he needs to eventually become a great architect. Thus, between infancy and adolescence, when he is a child—before labor laws were passed, in 1938, prohibiting the employment of youths, under 16 years of age—he is able to work, in the *Fountainhead*. Since the novel begins in 1922 when Roark is twenty-two. Yet he works a decade before then, starting in 1912. Since he decides, at ten years old, to renovate the earth with his unique structures. Just like Rand decided to be an author at 9 years old. Ergo, in the novel's literary universe, which corresponds to Rand's actual biography, Roark begins work in 1912. Deciding at ten that he wants to recreate the earth with his unique buildings. From a tender age, then, Roark dedicates his life to Architecture, to realize his dreams for himself, so he can actualize his building vision for the world. Because he knows, almost immediately, what he wants from his life. Then he goes about getting it. In-line with his aspirations for himself.

Indeed, Roarks early experiences, on the job and in school, coupled with his ability to take steps to realize want he wants from his life, early on, signals to readers that they can also form and realize their own purpose in their own lives.

For just like Roark works, "since childhood," as a builder, starting from the simplest jobs, in construction—such as rock-splitter, bolt-catcher, and errand-boy, "anything he can get,"— eventually graduating to higher-waged occupations, such as a plasterer, a plumber, and a steel worker—readers can likewise climb the rungs of their own careers, by first working a series of entry level jobs in their own professions (14). So they can then qualify for higher-level jobs in their unique vocations. For just like Roark first gains practical experience by working various construction gigs on different job sites – then learns the theory of how to build in *Architectural School* – the reader can also complement their early jobs with formal schooling. So they can also complement their on-the-job training with a university education.

Additionally, just like Roark builds a design portfolio for himself by sketching drawings of modern buildings, readers can also build a portfolio for themselves by visually representing on paper a wholistic view of their own professions. By also assembling a portfolio of poetry, if they want to be a poet, or news articles, if they want to be a journalist, or sample paintings, if they want to be an artist, or business plans, if they want to be a businessman. Thereby building a successful life for themselves by combining the best works of their specific professions. So they can present it later. So they can show potential employers, during job interviews, what they can do, not just what experience they have, or who they know. Further, just like Roark supplements his design folder by depicting line drawings, in school, in response to his assignments, and during his free time, readers can also build-up their professional portfolios before they even begin their formal work lives. So they are well ahead of the curve when they actually start looking for a job.

Moreover, just like Roark couples job skills he has learned on various construction sites with realizations he has made as a pupil, readers can also bring their own unique vision of their fields to the attention of prospective employers. By drawing on their previous workplace and schooltime experiences. Additionally, just like Roark combines lessons about the "efficiency of columns and panels under compression loads;" with lessons about the "torsion, flexibility, [and ruggedness of] flexible [building] materials"; with lessons about the "mechanical strength [of how different metals]" perform under various conditions; with lessons about "the agency of the laws of science" in application to "elastic structures;" readers can also develop their technical skills by also applying specific lessons they have learned on-the-job and at school to their specific working portfolios (Gordon, 10, 17, 20, 28, 23). So they have something to show potential employers when they begin their specific careers. Moreover, just like Roark creates a visual ideology that shows how light plastics, carbon fibers, and metal fabrics, can be blended together to create houses, skyscrapers, warehouses, and factories, the reader can also create their own unique system-of-ideas regarding the optimal practice of their own work. And, finally, just like Roark creates a visual philosophy that shows hiring managers how hard, rigid, materials, such as steel, concrete, and stone can be woven together, with malleable substances, to create elastic structures, the reader can also start their professional careers by designing a folio for themselves.

Similarly, readers can also seek out and work for a mentor, after graduating, just like Roark does. A mentor who will take them under his wing to further refine their professional expertise. And if readers find that their mentors are no longer working, then they can find a way to stay in their professions, by diligently applying elsewhere. Even if their employment ends with a particular boss.

For just like Roark stays the course, in his field of professional endeavor, by working as a civil field engineer, for a classical architect named Guy Francon [16], readers can also build a career for themselves, by working jobs that are at least partially in-line with what they want to

---

[16]   Thus, Roark is happy to inspect Francon's buildings, in the technical sense, in civil engineering terms. So he learns how to build structures that stand upright, since he wants to learn what makes different types of buildings stand. Roark is also happy to work in the engineering department of Francon's office, drafting schematic blueprints, for the firm. Since such an occupation, though not ideal, enables him to stay in architecture and make some survival money, as well. So he can live. It also enables him to further refine—at least on some level—his technical building skills.

do. For just like Roark still works for Guy Francon, even though he only enjoys the engineering aspects of his job, he does what he must to gain beneficial employment experience in architecture. Instead of going into another line-of-work because he cannot find the perfect job. Similarly, readers who want to advance their careers, may also find that sometimes they might have to do things they do not actually like all that much. In order to stay in their professions. But that eventually they can find the right job for them. One that fully utilizes their creative abilities. Even if temporarily some of what they are expected to do does not suit them that much.

That said, however, Roark's ultimate firing from Francon's office because he refuses to design the *Frink National Bank* building in line with Guy's wishes, shows readers that sometimes it is better to resign, or by fired by a company, and look for a job elsewhere, then to work a job that violates your identity. Since it is better to be let go, and find gainful employment elsewhere, than to stagnate in an unchallenging role, that does not align with who a person is nor what they can do.

This, ultimately, is why when Roark is fired by Francon, he stays what he is – instead of becoming something else – by seeking employment that suits him better. To do this he systematically makes a "list of architects whose work he resents the least." (92). Then he pounds the pavement, with his resume in hand, to find another job. Hoping that another builder will hire him because of his outstanding abilities. After getting interviews with a variety of different anonymous architects, he gets a range of retorts, declinations, and amused reactions, from them. Some architects are sad for him because his candor is touching. Other architects are actually happy that Roark seeks them out, and tries to work for them. Even though they don't hire him. Because it makes them suddenly proud of their own careers. Since they weathered the storm to make something of themselves, and their lives, while sadly Roark has no chance to flourish. Other architects who interview Roark are offended by his naïve ambition to originate a new building ideology. Because they were unable to do so. Other architects do not even look at Roark's sketches, because they are so worn down, by life, that they cannot by bothered, with a screwy architect, who is a total nothing, in their eyes. A terrible draftsman who was expelled from architectural school, worked for a crackpot lunatic named Henry Cameron, could not retain employment, with Guy Francon, for a steady length of time. And is thus, a complete loser, to them.

Yet, despite all of the hostile reactions, from employers, who neither understand Roark, nor objectively assess him, nor comprehend what he can do, Roark does not let their negative estimation of him taint his self-confidence. For Roark knows that he is a skilled architect, even if others do not realize this. Thus, he does not get discouraged by other people's rejections. Nor does he conform his soul to suit them. Rather, Roark looks for opportunities to shine, even if he has to play by their rules for a while. Similarly, readers can also do what they must, to find temporary jobs. Until they create a better opportunity for themselves down the road. Even if they are temporarily stuck in stagnant jobs for a bit.

For even though Roark ultimately feels that he must return to the same places, that rejected him earlier, because he goes broke, over the summer months, he is still not demoralized by the job search. Despite hearing the same robotic bromides from hiring managers. That he was "kicked out of Stanton [and booted] out of Francon's office" so he should not even waste their time (93). That, in effect, he should get out of their offices, and never come back, because he is not wanted.

However, after being spurned, rejected, declined, and patronized, by several different architects—on baseless grounds that he is not the right fit for them—Roark finds one glimmer of hope. He reads a rousing article in the *Architectural Tribune* titled *Make Way for Tomorrow*. Which gives Roark some hope that he will be hired for his merits – based on his talents – even though he is despised by some, shunned by others, ignored by the majority, and pitied by the rest. Roark feels this way because he is inspired by Prescott's article. Since he is moved by statements in it: about the difficulty of finding new talent in the field; about the many "great gifts" that have gone unnoticed in the field; about the many young talents that have been "lost in the struggle;" about "a lack of new blood, and new thought," in the discipline, which ultimately translates into a "lack of originality, vision, and courage" in architecture (93). Roark is also enthused when Prescott suggests that orthodox architecture is mainly comprised of traditional architects, with classical ideas, who have established an almost impenetrable old-boy network. Elite builders who bar entry into the field because they desperately cling to preserving the *status quo ante* in the building trades. Even though the discipline needs revitalization. Roark is particularly happy that Prescott's aim is to search for "promising beginners, to encourage them" to grow, to hone their skills and talents, and to "give them the chance they deserve" (93). Sadly, though this article has a tone of true authenticity, Roark discovers that Prescott does not really believe what he writes. Because Prescott does not reward young visionaries, such as Roark, for designing original buildings. For though Prescott thinks that Roark's buildings are "shocking and interesting", he does not think that they are "mature, focused, and disciplined" (94). Rather he thinks that Roark's drawings transmit originality for originality's sake" (94). Because even though Prescott thinks Roark's drawings are surprising and stimulating, he does not think they are in the spirit of the present day. Instead of hiring him, then, Prescott thinks that Roark needs to grow-up, to mature, to train himself in the ways of master architects, by fusing his modern sensibilities to classical art. This, then, is why Prescott hires a young beginner who has never "worked before" (94). Because this greenhorn merges a house that looks like "a grain silo," with an "emaciated" representation "of the *Parthenon*" (94). Evidently, Prescott hires this novice builder, over Roark, because this youth is willing to copy-cat buildings that Prescott wants erected. Instead of creating his own unique vision. What's even more surprising is that Prescott hires this young man over Roark even though this young man has never worked before. Even though this young man does he have a design portfolio. While Roark has both. However, Prescott hires him, because he wants to pretend, to his friends and collogues, that he is willing to give a young person a chance to be employed by a top architectural firm, because he has a generous soul. So that ultimately, he impresses his colleagues with his *largesse* instead of actually having a liberal spirit.

What is important, here, for readers to understand is that though they may encounter hiring managers, in their lives, who pretend to be idealistic, when they are not, it does not really matter too much. As long

CRITICAL ESSAYS ON AYN RAND'S THE FOUNTAINHEAD

as readers know who they are, what they want, and what they can do, that is all that matters.

Thus, it does not matter too much to Roark that he has to take a job with another posturing architect named John Erick Synte [17]. Since Roark feels that though working for Synte is not perfect, at least at Synte's firm, he will be permitted to design his own buildings, in his own way. Without any sort of interference, whatsoever. At least initially. Even though later he knows that his modern designs will be warped to fit Synte's eclectic philosophy. But because Roark feels confident that he *will* be able to design his own way at Synte's it does not matter too much that his designs will be violated later. Thus, Roark is not off-put that Synte amalgamates incongruous styles together into a disjunctive farrago. In order to impress Synte's colleagues, his clients, and the general public, more broadly. Since working for Synte will give Roark some of what he wants from his career.

Significantly, Roark's experience working for Synte, shows readers, that they should temporarily take jobs, that at least align with some of what they want, or most of what they want, if they can work those jobs in

---

[17] To explain, during Roark's interview, Synte glances at Roark's drawings, pronounces them to be radical and remarkable and offers a job to Roark. Because Synte is looking for a good *Modernist* architect, who will complement his eclectic building method. Since he already has *Classic*, *Gothic*, *Renaissance*, and *Miscellaneous*, architects working under his umbrella. But he needs a modernist architect under his belt. To balance the genres of architects he already has. Precisely, because modernism is now popular with the public and therefore must be represented in Synte's practice. So Synte can gain prestige, amongst his collogues, earn status, with the A.G.A, gain social respect, from the general public, and net money, from his clients. To fill the modernist void in his practice, then, Synte searches for a good modern designer. For his practice would be lacking without one. Therefore, Synte is delighted, when Roark finds him because he no longer needs to seek a Modernist Architect out. A good one has already found him. Thus, Synte is happy that Roark joins the team. Since Snyte's method of design depends on his 5 architects drawing sketches of their buildings, completely independently, in their own genres, or styles. After which, Synte chooses the sketch that is most apt for the building he has in mind. As the core, winning design, of the contests he stages. After which he blends together, suitable elements, of all the other sketches. For Synte's building philosophy is that six minds working together, in a synthetic style, is better than one mind working alone, in his own style. Because it will produce the kind of amalgamated structures that he wants to appease the general public. While one mind working alone won't.

good conscience. Since, if they do, they can later create their own perfect dream job, by using the experience they gained elsewhere to create their own optimal jobs. If, that is, there is no perfect job exists out there that currently exists that permits them to reach their highest potential by best voicing who they are.

After Roark's 5-month stint working for Synte, he gets his first client, Austen Heller. Since Heller likes, and thus only wants, the seaside house that Roark designs for him. Not the house with red brick walls; tiny windows; squashed spaces; small balconies; and broken pediments that Synte later designs for him. Rather, by restoring his original design of the *Heller House* Roark shows Heller that he does not have to put up with Synte's gross distortions of his house. That actually the domicile looks and functions better with stone native to the *Connecticut* seashore instead of unnatural red-brick; with large plexiglass panoramic windows instead of tiny shuttered windows; with projecting wings that sprawl out from the home's central building instead of a large colonial block house; with a great cantilevered terrace projecting over the sea instead of a tiny *Florentine* balcony; with a simple, utilitarian, entrance, instead of a flashy entryway, with unnecessary Greek ornaments; with a flat, simple, roof, that can be used as a terrace, instead of a steeped, gambrel roof, with a creaky weather vane. Indeed, by re-creating Heller's dream house before his very eyes, Roark does not unethically steal Heller away from Synte as some people think. Rather, he simply brings his architectural vision to Heller's attention. Leaving it to Heller to decide whether he wants to hire him, or not. Evidently, Heller wants to hire Roark to design his house because only Roark can create his dream house. This is why he winks at Roark, asks him to a business lunch, then writes him a $500 check. So Roark can go out on his own.

Here, what readers should understand from Roark's interaction with Austen Heller, is that typically fortune rewards bold individuals, who take calculated risks, to achieve their own visions. Since Roark risked it all, to make Heller his client. Instead of working a job that ultimately frustrated his identity. For Roark was not willing to perpetually work for a person who repeatedly disfigured his work. Rather, Roark seized an opportunity to create his own private practice. Similarly, readers, can also become solo-preneurs, if necessary, by creating employment that will make them happy with their professions.

Anyway, after the Heller episode, Roark goes into private practice, opens his own office, and starts building private residences, such as a gas station for a hard-working capitalist named Jimmy Gowan, a country residence for a noted industrialist named Mr. Sanborn, and sundry other small projects, as well. However, after the money [18] he has earned on these commissions dwindles, Roark slogs on. He keeps at it. He does not become discouraged that business is slow. He does not get demoralized that he lacks clients. He does not get dejected that nobody wants him. He does not become doubtful of his modern style because other people fault it. For Roark knows that his buildings are good; that his artistry is excellent; that his designs are wonderful; and that ultimately, he will succeed, despite his minor set-backs, stumbling blocks, and petty failures, along the way. Thus, even though Roark does not find any other "chances, offers, prospects, or commissions" in the winter of 1928; even though Roark is broke most of the time; even though Roark faces ideological challenges to his method of design; he refuses to adulterate his artistic integrity for anyone. (173). Neither by designing classical buildings for men like Robert L. Munday, who want him to betray his modernist calling in life by conforming his vision to their desires, nor by designing a *Gothic* bank for the executive board of the *Janss-Stuart* real estate company. For Roark will not corrupt his modern architectural philosophy by either cow-towing to the arbitrary whims of the *Janss-Stuart* real estate company's board nor by re-producing a traditional *Georgia Plantation* house that Munday delivered merchandise to when he was young. Rather, instead of giving Aquitania's executive board the safe Gothic building that it wants, Roark tries to get the *Janss-Stuart* real estate company to accept his radical modernist vision for their

---

[18] Evidently, Roark's primary value is not money. But building excellence. Accordingly, he pays for improvements to the *East Wing* of the *Sanborn House,* from his own pocket. Even though these improvements offset the entire commission he collects at the end of the project. He does this because Roark not only views houses as living organisms, that must be made perfect, but also because he wants to create the best houses possible. Domiciles that will bring him his kinds of clients.

firm's headquarters. Similarly, instead of building a conformist *Georgia Plantation* for Mr. Munday, that symbolizes other people's victory over him, Roark decline this client on principle. Because it violates his identity. Thus, if Roark, at first, cannot get the prospective clients, or projects, that he wants, he tries to get these clients to recognize what the best is. By trying to persuade them that he can build for them "the most comfortable, the most logical, the most beautiful house that can be built" (14). But if he can't convince clients about the desirability of their new home, Roark does his own thing by going his own way. Instead of violating his artistic principles by working a distorting job.

However, because Roark wants to stay in private architectural practice, instead of smashing boulders in a rock quarry, his final glimmer of hope to achieve this goal now, rather than later, is to design a *Manhattan Bank*, purely in a modernistic sky-scraper style. Yet, unbeknownst to Roark Toohey orchestrates this commission, so Roark buckles to the board's demands to add "a simplified Doric portico," at the building's front entrance, "a cornice on top" of the building, and "a stylized Greek ornament," on the side of the building (195). If he wants the commission. However, Roark does not yield to Toohey's schemes to "collectivize all [the visual] arts" by not buckling to Toohey's effort to gain total control over architecture (Journals, 215). By not subordinating himself to Toohey's yes men. Instead, Roark would rather labor in an obscure, far-flung rock quarry, waiting for an opportunity to resume building his own way. Rather than to prostitute his designs for anyone. Even rich and powerful people. Ergo, despite having a meagre $14.57 cents in his wallet, Roark does not trade his soul for money. Even though he desperately needs funds. Since Roark's happiness is the goal of his life. Not dollars. Thus, Roark must either build buildings his own way, by persuading his types of clients to hire him, or not build, at all.

This is why Roark hammers stones in a rock quarry, in the Summer of 1928, for $1.63 dollars an hour. Until he can save enough money to resume his career as a professional architect. Which opportunity, he gets, after a businessman, named Roger Enright, summons him back to *New York City* to design a radical apartment building for him called the *Enright House*. Evidently, Roark's patience pays off. Since the events of the story shows that he was right not to take the *Manhattan Bank* job; that he was right not to yield to Mr. Munday; that he was right not to succumb to the Janss-Stewart real estate company. Since he got clients buildings without having to conform to their capricious building standards. And though Roark's path was much more difficult because he elected to go it alone, instead of conforming to society, ultimately, his life was much more rewarding for having chosen to live out his own values. Since by maintaining his artistic principles Roark won the right to create unified buildings all of one style. His own.

Likewise, readers should also understand, that sometimes, in life, the best path is not always the easiest one. That sometimes, going it alone, by doing your own thing, even though very challenging, can ultimately yield a better result for you and your life.

If Roark conformed by always working cookie-cutter jobs for traditional architects, like Guy Francon or John Erik Synte, or if he twisted his soul by designing conventional buildings for conformist clients, like Mrs. Sanborn, or Mr. Sutton, or if Roark caved to financial pressures by designing a mongrel *Manhattan Bank* building for Mr. Weidler, he would not be the great modern architect that he is in the novel. Nor would Enright have selected him to design a revolutionary apartment building for him in the center of *Manhattan*. Since Roark would not have the maverick buildings necessary to draw Enright's attention to him in the first place.

Similarly, Roark does not conform to society by networking through *Kiki Holcombe's* architectural salon. Since Roark does not toady before anyone during Kiki's *soirees* just to get their business. Rather, Roark build the *Cord Building*, in the Center of *Manhattan*, the *Aquitania Hotel*, on *Central Park South*, followed by the *Stoddard Temple*, overlooking the *Hudson River*. Instead of ass-kissing Kiki's prestigious clientele.

However, because Roark is creating a solid reputation for himself as an excellent builder, despite Toohey best efforts to stop him, this last building, the *Stoddard Temple*, is actually an exquisite trap, that Toohey sets for Roark. So he does not thwart Toohey's bid to control the field. But is instead relegated to perform obscure work, in far flung places, like *Clayton Ohio*. To repeat, the *Stoddard Temple*, is Toohey's masterfully orchestrated, elaborate ploy, to drive Roark into obscurity, by turning religionists against him. So Toohey can dominate architecture and ultimately society. This, then, is why Toohey tells Hopton Stoddard to tell Roark to build a monument to the human spirit that expresses the "essence of all religion," which is "the great aspiration of the human spirit to reach towards the highest, the noblest, and the best" (327). Here, Toohey coaches Stoddard to say this, so that Roark, an arch atheist, builds the temple in the first place. So that Toohey can entrap him later. For Toohey knows that this line of reasoning will work on Roark. Because Toohey knows that though Roark does not believe in God, he does believe that human beings should celebrate themselves, in their own way, by realizing the best within them. Ergo, not only does Toohey coach Stoddard on what to say to Roark—to prime Roark to accept the *Stoddard Temple*—he also insists that Stoddard not tell Roark that he Toohey is involved in the project in anyway. Lest Roark decline the project. On grounds that Toohey is up to something. Further, Toohey persuades Stoddard to erect a high screened fence, around the temple, so nosy reporters do not report on its construction prematurely. Then, Toohey instructs Stoddard to hire an army of press agents to hype the temple. So that on reveal day, the impact is severe. So that when the temple is publicly shown, religionists, from all creeds, faiths, and backgrounds will vociferously object to Roark's temple on grounds of blasphemy. Thereby, scandalizing Roark further in newspapers, in court, amongst the general populas, and amongst outraged people, who all hiss their resentment, at him, for violating their spiritual faith.

What readers should understand about Toohey's trap, is that it is possible for people to come back from a solid defeat, to eventually achieve success. If they keep at it.

For even though Roark is relegated to constructing small homes in the ensuing years "one in *Pennsylvania* and one near *Boston*," he does not feel that they are "unimportant," like Dominique does. Because any building project is worthwhile, to Roark, because each structure poses unique challenges that he loves to solve (479). This, then, is why Roark says that though the houses were "inexpensive," to build they were "very interesting to do" because each building, to Roark is unique, and thus teaches him something about how to build better (479). And though Dominique thinks that these small domiciles are comparatively insignificant—after Roark created structures like the "Enright House," or the "Cord Building,"—he does not "think of [them] that way" (480). Because he "loves" constructing any building, even the most modest one, because "every building [to him] is like a person, single and unrepeatable" (480). At this rejoinder, Dominique wonders if Roark will be "doing five-story buildings for the rest of [his] life" (480). Such as *Janer's Department Store*, for example, which to her is in some *Podunkan* "hole of a place," like Clayton Ohio (480). But Roark does not think so. He just thinks that Clayton is a small provincial town in rural America. In sum, Roark enjoys every building that he undertakes, because each building gives him more experience in designing and constructing buildings in his own way. Thus, he is prepared to labor in relative obscurity, for the rest of his life, "if necessary" (480). However, he "do[es] not think it will be like that" (480). Because he'll find a better job, one day. Since he knows how to do so much.

Roark's right. Ultimately, his strategic patience, pays off. Because a fraudster, named Caleb Bradley, "who made a fortune in Florida real estate during the State's housing boom," wiggles out of the dark corner, he was hiding in, eversince, to select an unsociable architect, like Roark [19], to build a summer resort that nobody will go to (531). So he can embezzle investor funds. Because Bradley's criminal scheme depends on him building a vacation resort that will fail. That he can bilk money from. For Mr. Bradley sells 200 % of *Monadnock* hoping to steal his investors' money when the resort tanks. However, the resort does not fail. Quite the opposite. It is a rousing success. That puts Roark back on top of the

---

[19] Importantly, Roark does not collude with Bradley, in anyway whatsoever, to build Monadnock. He is simply selected by Bradley, to build Monadnock, because Bradley thinks that he is a scandalous architect, that most people hate. Ergo, Bradley hopes that the few people who find out about Monadnock, will choose to boycott the resort, on principle. Since in Bradley's mind, religionists, especially Christians, will refuse to stay at the resort, because it was built by an alleged hater of religion, who was recently excoriated over the Stoddard Temple fiasco. And, since America, had more serious, spiritual values, during the 1930's, when the novel was set, and in 1943, when the novel was published, Roark's construction of the Stoddard Temple, was more of an offense, to the moral majority of people, with religious Christian sensibilities.

building trades. Since businessman hire Roark, from then on, because he can make money for them under nearly impossible odds.

Ergo, due to Roark's rising wave of newfound popularity, he is selected, in the spring of 1936, to design a building, for the *March of the Centuries World Fair*, with 8 other architects. But again, Roark will not trade his artistic soul by conforming his designs to the distortions of others. Rather, he takes pride in designing unique buildings that have integrity, just like he does. Thus, despite many different attempts to get Roark to conform, he does not give up who he is, nor what he wants, to please others. Rather, Roark's tenacious drive to build buildings his own way ultimately leads to his stunning success.

Thus, Roark's formative architectural purpose early in life; his youthful jobs in the construction trades; his formal schooling which educates him further; his ability to find a mentor, who can guide him further; his dedication to producing values in architecture; his professional integrity that only permits him to work certain types of jobs, for certain types of people, at certain organizations; his bold initiative to create opportunities for himself; his uncompromising nature that never allows him to betray his core principles; his willingness to take small building jobs so he can remain in his field; his total disregard for the evaluations of *most* others; his introspective self-mastery that makes him know himself; his personal recognition of the basic goodness of another human being, transmits several good morals to readers. One, it shows readers that they should find their purpose early in life, the earlier the better, and take immediate steps, to realize their ambitions. Two, it shows readers that they can work a sequence of entry level jobs in their fields, when they are young, to learn the basic skills that they need to advance in their chosen professions. Three, it shows readers that after working in high school, as a teenager, in their selected trade, they can then enroll, in a fitting university, if appropriate, to *extract* from that institution, what they need to know. Four, it shows readers that after college, they can seek out, and find a mentor, who can teach them what they want to know, in their particular line-of-endeavor. Five, it shows readers that they should not let their professional rejections, demoralize them, discourage them, or make them doubt themselves. Because every life, even the best life, Roark shows, is beset by failures, frustrations, and difficulties. Six, it shows readers that while they should have firm, long-term, principles that they should not compromise on, it is possible to co-operate with like-minded others, in certain situations, to realize a specific goal. Seven, it shows readers that sometimes they should put it all on the line by boldly pursuing their professional goals, even if doing so risks their dismissal. Eight, it shows readers that they should ignore the slander, the aspersions, the character attacks, and the gossip mongering, of unthinking, or mean-spirited, others by ignoring naysayers altogether. So they can pursue their career ambitions by remaining true to who they are. Nine, it shows readers that even if they achieve success, by meriting money, or gaining power, or both, never should they let their accomplishments change who they are. And, ten, it shows readers that they should pursue their career ambitions, persistently and indefatigably, regardless of what anyone else says, does, or thinks, is best.

Moreover, the real-world linkage between Howard Roark and Ayn Rand, ultimately shows readers that to build a successful joyous life for themselves, that brings them money, power, and fame, as a secondary by product of their intellectual accomplishments, a person must construct their lives like a good novel. Where each event leads to the next, in a logical manner, according to a proper sequence of affairs, characterized by a rising action, a coherent denouement, and an ultimate resolution. Because a person's ultimate success in life depends on how intelligently they focus, throughout their differing lives, how hard they work, in their specific careers, and how bold they are, in their manner of creation.

So that individuals, in the general culture, also realize their ideal, or real, selves by living out who they are in-line with their own moral vision of the good life. And a good life, Roark shows, consists of having positive moral aspirations for yourself, of acting with principled integrity in your life, of creating positive values in your profession, of respecting morally good people in this world, of being happy with what you have accomplished with your time, and of always maintaining who you are in reality. Further, Roark's life also shows readers that when they strive for their own happiness—by living out their one main passion, in life—it is possible for them to reach excellence.

REFERENCES

Bayer, J.B. (2007). The Fountainhead and the Spirit of Youth. (pp.227-242). In Essays on Ayn Rand's the Fountainhead. Ed. Robert Mayhew. Lanham, MD: Lexington Books.

Berliner, M.S. (Ed). (1995). *Letters of Ayn Rand*. New York City, New York: Penguin Books.

Bernstein, A. (2000). *Cliff Notes on Rand's The Fountainhead*. New York: Houghton Mifflin Harcourt.

Bernstein, A. (2007). Understanding the Rape Scene in the Fountainhead. (pp. 201-208). In Essays on Ayn Rand's the Fountainhead. Ed. Robert Mayhew. Lanham, MD: Lexington Books.

Boeckman, T. (2007). *The Fountainhead as a Romantic Novel*. (pp. 119-153). In Essays on Ayn Rand's the Fountainhead. Ed. Robert Mayhew. Lanham, MD: Lexington Books.

Den-Uyl. D. (1950). *The Fountainhead an American Novel*. New York: Twayne Publishers.

Ghate, O. (1997). *The Basic Motivation of the Creators and the Masses in The Fountainhead. From Essays on Ayn Rand's The Fountainhead.* (pp. 243-279). Editor Robert Mayhew. Lexington Books. Lanham, Maryland: Rowman & Littlefield Publishers Inc..

Gordan, J.E. (2020). *Structures or Why Things Don't Fall Down*. New York: Hachette Books.

Gurgen, Emre (2021). *The Fountainhead Reference Guide: A to Z (Narrative Version 2ⁿᵈ Edition)*. Illinois: AuthorHouse.

Harriman, D. (Ed.) (1999). *Journals of Ayn Rand*. New York: Plume.

Kline, W. (2016). Identity, Professional Ethics, and Substantive Style in the Fountainhead. In Capitalism and Commerce in Imaginative Literature: Perspectives on Business from Novels and Plays. Ed. Edward W. Younkins. (pp.287-303). Lanham, MD: Lexington Books.

Milgram, S. (2007). The Fountainhead from Notebook to Novel: The Composition of Ayn Rand's First Ideal Man (pp.3-40). In Essays on Ayn Rand's the Fountainhead. Ed. Robert Mayhew. Lanham, MD: Lexington Books.

Milgram, S. (2007). Three Inspirations for the Ideal Man: *Cyrus Paltons, Enjolras, and Cyrano de Bergerac* (By Shoshana Milgram) (pp.177-199). In Essays on Ayn Rand's the Fountainhead. Ed. Robert Mayhew. Lanham, MD: Lexington Books.

Rand, A. (1997). Harriman, D. Ed. *Journals of Ayn Rand*. New York: Plume Books.

Smith, T. (2007). Unborrowed Vision: Independence and Egoism in The Fountainhead. (pp. 285-304). In Essays on Ayn Rand's the Fountainhead. Ed. Robert Mayhew. Lanham, MD: Lexington Books.

ESSAY 3

Individualism & Capitalism Versus Collectivism & Communism in Ayn Rand's *The Fountainhead*

The Fountainhead not only elevates the morality of individualism and capitalism over the morality of collectivism and communism it shows the ultimate impact and consequences of both brought to their rational conclusions. If man lives for himself, Ayn Rand shows, and pursues his own values in a free nation, then he is happy and fulfilled. Conversely, if a man lives for some higher form of authority— such as God, the State, the nation, the folk, the community, the tribe, the class, the caste, the mob, or his neighborhood—then ultimately, he will not be happy. For depression, Ayn Rand argues, is what happens to a man when he alienates himself for a second-handed cause or being. Because when a man betrays his inner values to placate the masses—instead of following his own individual truth or vision—he makes himself miserable.

We see this manifestation in the character of Gail Wynand, for example, who is psychologically ruined, by then end of the novel, since he sold his soul to make money and gain power—by pandering constantly to the lowest tastes of the crowd for wealth and affluence. To explain, though Wynand thinks that he alone forms public opinion through his newspapers, he is dismayed to discover that he only controls the public so long as he says what the crowds want him to. Yet, when Wynand tries to promulgate his real values by defending Roark in the court of public opinion, he is shocked to discover that he does not hold "power over a collective [public] soul" as he thought (631). Rather it is the mob who rules and owns him. For Wynand's readers do not care that a genius, like Roark, has been violated. Instead, they protest Wynand's defense of Roark by boycotting his newspaper. This sudden discovery, in turn, utterly depresses Wynand. Since it makes him realize that he betrayed himself, and his deepest values, for riches only, not power. Wynand's lust for affluence also makes him suicidal during the beginning of the novel. For Wynand is introduced to readers in the desperate act of suicide, since he raises a gun to his temple to shoot himself in the head. Indeed, Wynand's forlorn mind state, signaled by his drive to exterminate himself, shows readers that he experiences enormous depression because he built his media empire by delivering people their vices, instead of writing from his own values. In fact, Wynand's type of "circulation-boosting" rabble rousing makes him an ethical collectivist, in spirit, who betrays his inner soul by pandering to the outer crowd. Yet by catering to the public's tastes Wynand abandons his right to form and defend his own values through journalism. Thus, because Wynand is not a principled journalist, like Austen Heller, but is instead an unscrupulous demagogue, like Ellsworth Toohey, he shows readers that one cannot be happy "without [a] self and pride in that self." (Rand, Journals, 91).

Further, because Wynand type second-handers confuse what capitalism really is in the general culture, Ayn Rand felt that she had to write a novel that undercut the idea that capitalists are vultures who enrich themselves by exploiting poor people. Rather, she creates a supporting ideology for capitalistic democracy through her characters, which is based on individualism, egoism, and selfishness. For Ayn Rand felt that such a free-market philosophy needed a fair hearing in the general culture, since such entrepreneurial values were not being expressed "elsewhere at that time in the literary, artistic, or political world" (Den Uyl, 14). Because the writings of the period largely denigrated American businessman as evil exploiters who bilk the indigent. Conversely, *The Fountainhead* celebrates capitalism and individualism, by voicing a newfound nationalism that expresses the original "founding principles of the United States—the sovereign right of the individual" (Bernstein, Cliff Notes, 46). For many characters in the novel, such as Roger Enright, for example, or Jimmy Gowan, for instance, are staunch individualists, who want to work for themselves by creating their own businesses. Because they have the spirit of a capitalist. Specifically, Jimmy Gowan is an auto-mechanic, who after fifteen years of back-breaking work is ready to go out on his own to open a gas station, while Roger Enright is a coal miner, who saves enough money to open an oil business, "a publishing house, a restaurant, a radio shop, an [auto]-garage, [and] a plant manufacturing electric refrigerators" (256). Evidently, both of these men are true capitalists who earn their money *not* by cheating the downtrodden. But by providing beneficial goods and services at an affordable price. Thus, the portrait of these two hard working Americans shows readers that "capitalism [not only] makes us wealthier [and] better off [if we] live according to the sorts of 'selfish' principles that are good for (that is, suited to) human life" but also that *Capitalism* rewards a man's spirit if he is an original entrepreneurial thinker with a bold commercial spirit. (Den Uyl, 14).

Yet, to Ayn Rand, corrupt journalists, like Gail Wynand, do not represent real *Capitalism*, nor free enterprise, in its true sense. Since Wynand made his money by exploiting public trends, and pandering to the masses, while true capitalists are "originators and innovators who [go] *against* the masses, against all public opinion, against all 'trends' and 'currents' " (Letters, 224). Specifically, because Wynand creates a newspaper, a magazine, and a tabloid syndicate that originates and nurtures collective media vice; instead of creating a media empire that creates and fosters individual journalistic values; he represents to Ayn Rand the men who are destroying free enterprise today.

Besides showing readers that by bucking the *status quo* the best men under capitalism, like Howard Roark, are usually opposed by most of humanity, *The Fountainhead* also shows readers that though "under modern capitalism [the] best man [usually] win[s]" this fact is "not as important as the [idea] that [in a] capitalistic democracy there is [an objective] *best*." (Journals, 105). This, then, is what *The Fountainhead* exemplifies. That capitalism not only rewards people for their brilliant entrepreneurship by making them rich, but, more largely, that there is a best way to do things, which usually pits the innovative entrepreneur against a staunchly conservative "hostile" society inimical to their flourishing.

To explain, Toohey opposes people, like Howard Roark, who are true capitalists, because he jockeys for power through the promotion of a collectivist economy. So he can ultimately control humanity's spirit by leashing its' economics. Thus, Toohey purposefully "subordinates the spiritual to the economic, in proclaiming the dependence of the spirit upon the material," since he hopes to collectivize the nation by showing people that their psychic needs can only be met through a collective economy (Rand, Journals, 107). Thus, everything Toohey does, says, and thinks, throughout the novel, is geared towards establishing a spiritual form of ethical collectivism right here in America: A type of economic group-think, if you will, that subordinates, or alienates, the individual to the masses. He does this in a number of ways. One, he is a vocational adviser in an unnamed *New York* university, where he advises his students to not purse their spiritual passions – as they want to. But to pursue, instead, a practical profession that they can be "calm, sane, and matter-of-fact [about] even if they hate it." (300). Ultimately, Toohey says this so his students become socially minded state citizens concerned with the welfare of the community; not selfish capitalists. Two, while advising, Toohey not only reviews books, plays, and art exhibitions for a series of socialist magazines (i.e. *New Voices*; *New Pathways*; *New Horizons*; and, finally, *New Frontiers*) he also lectures in front of small audiences, in obscure forums, where he argues that humanity needs to originate and deploy a comprehensive form of collectivist ethics, which can most easily be achieved through a collective economy. Here, Toohey realizes that if he can "take control of humanity's economics—[which is] concrete and accessible—[he] can hope to control humanity's spirit" (Rand, Journals, 107). Three, Toohey pens a book named *Sermons in Stone*, in which he not only tries to collectivize architecture by glorifying the contributions of the common man to the art but he also writes this book to "discredit the significance of individuals in history in favor of the economic significance of the masses." (Journals, 107). This, then, is how Toohey explodes the concept of capitalism amongst his readers by casting doubt over a free market system in which a country's trade and industry are transacted by private owners who work for their own profits, rather than controlled by a centralized State that mandates that a person must devote their profits to the social welfare of others. Four, Toohey writes a syndicated *Daily Banner* column, called *One Small Voice*, where he concerns himself **not** with the individual creation of great artists and capitalists. But with the collectivistic production of bad artists and socialists who all express, in their works, a virulent form of group-think dedicated to the destruction of individual greatness. Five, Toohey subtly spreads anti-capitalist messages in the Wynand papers by writing that people's "personal motive[s] are always 'goaded by selfishness' or 'egged on by greed.'" (615). He also arranges for *the Banner's* "crossword puzzles [to define] 'capitalists' as 'obsolescent individuals'" (615). In so doing, Toohey popularizes a newfangled form of anti-capitalist slang that is anti-mind and anti-reason. Six, Toohey arranges for an outstanding *Banner* drama critic named Jimmy Kearns [20] to be replaced by his hand-picked stooge named Jules Fougler. Since his plot to take over the *Banner* depends on him being able to control the scene unopposed. Seven, Toohey creates a *Union of Wynand Employees*, who collectively walk out on Wynand during the *Banner* strike. So they can make Wynand realize that no one man can run a capitalistic business on his own by dictating editorial policy. That, conversely, the *Banner's* editors, writers, copy readers, proof readers and slotmen must have "some say in running [a newspaper] where [they] make [their] living" (676). By having his proxies say this Toohey infers that economic and ethical individualism fosters a sense of human depravity. Eight, Toohey denigrates capitalism's financial instruments, like the institution of private inheritance, for example, or the possession of private property, for instance, by not only turning over a $100, 000 check bequeathed to him to the *Workshop of Social Studies*—"a progressive institute of [higher]-learning where he [holds] the post of lecturer on *Art as a Social Symptom*"—but also by defining marriage to be an old-fashioned economic device designed to perpetuate the institution of private property (225). Nine, Toohey delivers a rousing speech to a striking labor union, so he can unite and rule a mass of collectivized people, who all think that capitalism and individualism are evil social

---

[20] **Jimmy Kearns** is a "bright kid, the best drama critic in town," who analyzes plays for Wynand's *Daily Banner* (475). But because he is "smart as a whip" with a promising mind of his own, **Toohey wants to replace him** with one of his stooges, a yes-man named Jules Fougler. For **Toohey does not "want any whips around [the *Banner*] except the ones [that he] holds."** (475). Especially since his plot to take over the *Banner* depends on him being able to control the scene, unopposed. This, then, is why Alvah Scarret first fires Jimmy Kearns, then hires Jules Fougler to replace him. Because Toohey tells him to.

systems that crush the common man. In sum, by not only declaring the reliance of the spirit upon the material but also by clamoring for "a perfect form of ethical collectivism" in people's living and working lives, Toohey broadcasts the belief that group ethics are necessary for a collective economy (Rand, Journals, 85). Since he wants to herd America into neat groups of easily controllable people—milksops without a backbone—so Toohey can rule the world by dominating everybody.

Thus, to logic-chop the idea that individual artists can succeed in life by chasing profits, Toohey writes 8 articles in *One Small Voice* where he not only promotes moral collectivism over the individual creation of artists but where he also endorses a collective economy that is not based on *Capitalism's* selfish profit motive.

In his first article, then, named *Songs and Things*, Toohey denigrates any type of "for-profit" music produced alone by individuals; like solo operas, for instance, or singular classical performances, for example; proclaiming that "non-profit" folk-music is morally superior to it. Evidently, Toohey elevates music produced in groups over music created by individuals to repudiate the notion that a musician can flourish on his own under *Capitalism*.

In his second *Banner* article, Toohey further undermines the idea that an individualist artist can succeed by himself under *Capitalism* by mocking the idea that great artists, such as Steven Mallory, can create worthy sculptures of man. In this article, then, Toohey writes that Mallory's statues are bad primarily because they dispute the notion that "God created the world and the human form" (226). Here, Toohey assassinates the characters of great artists and sculptors who oppose his *collective* vision of mankind. So that he can champion a sense of group ethics in society by promoting collectivist artists of various sorts. Since Toohey wants the public to believe that sculptors, and other artists, can only succeed in life if they work well with others in a socialist setting. This, ultimately, is how Toohey promotes the virtue of social adaptability over the value of creating substantive products alone.

In his third article titled *Sacrilege*, Toohey criticizes Roark's *Stoddard Temple* by writing that his shrine to man's spirit is more akin to a "warehouse" or a "brothel" rather than a "great monument to religion"

(348, 349). Basically, Toohey writes this to not only show his readers that their spiritual religious values can also be expressed through the material—a temple—but also to explode the concept that individual artists can succeed by themselves in a capitalistic economy. For Toohey wants to expose individual artists, like Roark, to the censure of the people. For violating society's collectivized sense of religion. Conversely, Toohey celebrates in his *fourth Banner article*, the paintings created by the workers of *New York City's* sanitation department. To convey the impression that artists can only succeed in life if they band together in groups under a *Socialist-Marxist-Communist* economy.

To further discredit the notion that individualist artists can thrive by themselves, on their own terms, under capitalism, Toohey's sixth *Banner* article titled *I Swim With the Current*, tries to disassociate Roark's radical brand of modernist architecture from a broad popular movement. It does this by linking a talentless hack named *Gus Webb* to modern architecture *writ large*. Because *Webb* is someone whom Toohey can control. Since *Webb* is essentially Toohey's stoolie; a yes man who politically enacts Toohey's spiritual ideas of group-think. As a reward for his allegiance, then, Toohey enriches *Webb* by either giving him phony-modernist buildings to design, like the new plant of the *Bassett Brush Company*—which amplifies the "Grandeur of the Little"—or by ensuring that *Webb* participates in governmental buildings, such as the *Cortlandt Homes Housing Project*. (494). In sum, by turning his artistic follower and crony, a stoolie named *Gus Webb*, into modern Architecture's *de facto* representative, Toohey not only reasons that real modernist architects, like Cameron and Roark, should not be credited with creating and developing the movement, he also ensures that individualist architects who violate his collectivist principles do not see the light of day—at least for a while. Most importantly, Toohey shows readers that if he cannot eliminate a category of art he does not like he will simply take it over and corrupt it. Until people no longer know who represents the movement and thus what its characteristics are.

In brief, by pretending that the only solution to capitalism and individualism's evil moral code is socialism and communism's benevolent ethical ideology, Toohey tries to eradicate independent thinking in his followers, so they blindly follow his leadership. So they mindlessly follow the unthinking mentality necessary for him to rule. He does this by showing his followers that "it is not [just] the big capitalists and their money that he opposes; he opposes the faint conceptions of individualism still existing in society." (Rand, Journals, 107). For though businessmen and capitalists are also obnoxious to Toohey what is even worse to him are individualist thinkers who refuse to obey him. Because their counter-example of noncompliance undermines his ability to collectivize the arts. So he can become its' *de facto* dictator. But even though Toohey tries to discredit Roark by maligning his philosophic "first-principles" (i.e. individualism; selfishness; rationality; and egoism) Toohey's collectivist army of philosophers is still routed by Roark when Roark ignores their Toohey-inspired assaults against him.

Indeed, by disregarding the intense social opposition that Toohey pits against him—which Roark achieves by designing outstanding modernist buildings despite the public's outcry—he rises above the collectivized scandals organized against him. By proceeding with his usual architectural business anyway until his critics simply vanish away. For despite facing a whole host of attacks from artists, journalists, religionists, businessmen, and others, Roark still moves forward with, and achieves, his architectural plans. For Roark is such a resolute creator, with such a great mind, that he is able to succeed on his own terms by following his own vision. Thus, despite the malicious attacks that Toohey gathers and directs against him, Roark rises to success in his own way. By building his own unique structures. Which determination not only results in Roark realizing his primary goal of transforming the earth's surface with his structures but which drive ultimately causes him to "move ahead [and] carry the rest of mankind" with him. (Bernstein, 18).

Thus, to caution readers away from the *Intellectual Toohey's*, Ayn Rand wrote *The Fountainhead* to undercut America's imminent slide toward collectivism. Since during the late 1930's when the novel was written *America* was in danger of being swallowed by communism just like *Europe* was. Because in real life and in the universe of the book dictatorships threaten large portions of the world with their collectivist rule. Since in the decades between the two world wars "collectivism appeared to be on the threshold of military conquest of large portions of the globe." (Bernstein, Cliff Notes). To stop *America* from falling to this collectivist menace, then, Ayn Rand depicts a wide variety of rights-supporting characters acting in their own best interests. Men like Howard Roark, Austen Heller, Mike Donnigan, Steven Mallory, and Roger Enright, who transcend any efforts to absorb the *United States* into a collectivist dictatorship by living out who they are. Despite who agrees, or disagrees, with their thoughts and actions. Thus, by featuring a determined cast of individuals acting in their own best interests, Ayn Rand suggests that America will *not* fall to the socialist, communist, fascist, and religious dictatorships—and *theosophies*—made prevalent during the early decades of the twentieth century—any time soon. Because if America acts like Ayn Rand's heroes, the author infers that the nation will rise above and defeat men like Toohey. Thereby overcoming any despotic tyrants threatening it—"whether of the Communist, [military, or theocratic] varieties"—that had already conquered large portions of Europe between 1914 and 1948. (Bernstein, Cliff's Notes, 7). That were rapidly consuming the world at the time. In other words, Ayn Rand diminishes the ideological risk of America falling to one of these rising collectivist dictatorships through her fiction. By suggesting that if America fell to one of these nation-destroying governments that was poised on its' ideological doorstep then all people living in the *United States* were doomed to become slaves. Since their individual rights would be eliminated by an entrenched collectivist ruler who cares not about their individual liberties. Such as their freedom of speech, their property rights, their right to bear arms, and their right to assemble. But rather wants to collect their identities so he can establish a dictatorship right here in America.

Indeed, Ayn Rand defended the individual rights of *Americans* so strongly precisely because she experienced, in her own life, collectivism's social ills. Because "first the *Communists* [seized power in] her native *Russia* [under Joseph Stalin]; then the *Fascists* [rose] to power in *Italy*," under Benito Mussolini; and, finally, the "*National Socialists* took political control of *Germany*" under Adolf Hitler (Bernstein, Cliff Notes). Evidently, because Ayn Rand saw collectivism overwhelming the world during her life-time, she felt an urgent need to write a book, such as *The Fountainhead*, that shattered the concept of collectivism. Since she wanted to combat, in human and particular terms, the ideological underpinnings of group-think. Especially, because she was aware that before these collectivistic movements rose to power in the world there was already strong ideological and moral support for the *Communists*, the *Fascists*, and *even* the *Nazi's* in America. Because in the United States, *Communist*, *Fascist*, and *Nazi* societies were deemed "noble experiments" by many elements of the intelligentsia. Since many public intellectuals back then believed that an individual's duty was to *selflessly* serve the people, society, or the nation, instead of advancing his, or her, own selfish interests. This, then, is why many philosophers, authors, and critics, of those times believed that the rising collectivist trends of that era where actually good for humanity. Because they emphasized that a person's "moral responsibility is to his fellow man"—not to himself (Bernstein, Cliff Notes). Accordingly, many politicians, labor leaders, and even businessman of the early 1940's embraced collectivist social systems in their public speeches and writings. Since, at the time, collectivism seemed to be on the verge of bringing tremendous benefits to the world. This, ultimately, is why literary critics, professional artists, and the mainstream press of that epoch all embraced crowd pleasing notions: like the supremacy of the "working class," the rule of the "public interest," and the idea of subordinating yourself to something greater than yourself, like the "common good". This is also why the imaginative literature of the 1940's sympathized with ideas such as the reign of the "masses," the rule of the "welfare state," the authority of the "public interest," and the idea that "we are our brother's keepers." Because during the first half of the twentieth century, "collectivism—whether of a mild 'social democratic' variety or a more militant form of communism and socialism—was everywhere on the rise". (Den Uyl, 6). Since the climate of the period was largely devoid of individualist sentiments. Thus, to stave-off America's looming collapse into statism and full-collectivization, Ayn Rand shows the *Fountainhead's* readers that America must not succumb to the collectivist dictatorships that have already subjugated large parts of Europe to their despotic rule. She does this by having Toohey gloat that since "Europe [as already been] swallowed" by a gushing torrent of *collectivism*, it is only a matter of time until Americans will "stumble on to follow" (669). Toohey says this to not only show readers that America was ripe to fall to communism at the time, he also says this to project the consequences over the personal lives of the people if a *communist* dictatorship was established right here in America. So that readers not only oppose the doctrine that man should subordinate himself to an all-powerful state but also so that readers embrace the idea that they should live for themselves in a free country that protects their individual rights and private property.

This, then, is why Ayn Rand reasons that under capitalism, *all* men are free to choose their friends, their companions, and their business partners, based on mutual values. Instead of being compelled to forge social friendships based on identity politics: because the other person shares their same race, class, gender, ethnicity, or cultural background. In other words, since many of the *Fountainhead's* characters enter into different relationships freely of their own choice—based on sharing like values with a certain person—the book ultimately shows readers that under capitalism men are free to choose their colleagues, their companions, and who they will deal with in life. That, conversely, in a dictatorship, people are bound by the family, the tribe, and the caste they were born into. Since, during the early 1900's, human relationships, in these various dictatorships, was defined by "mutual suspiciousness, hostility, and cruelty, [since back then] everyone regarded his neighbor as a potential threat, and nothing was held more cheaply than human life." (Rand, Capitalism The Unknown Ideal, 323).

Yet Toohey's ultimate drive to unite the globe into a communist dictatorship encounters firm resistance by Americans, since in the *United States* Toohey faces a legacy of individualism and civil freedoms that collectivists in *Europe* would not. Since before the twentieth century the world had offered some degree of recognition for individual achievement; some amount of valuing of singular leaders; and some appreciation for people who are exceptions to the masses. Since, according to Ayn Rand, Americans, back then, still had "vestiges of respect for individualism ground into it by centuries of aristocracy." (Journals, 108). Thus,

Toohey's drive to create a communist world order—starting with the establishment of a *Marxist* dictatorship right here in America—is ultimately frustrated. Because in the modern context of the *United States*, Toohey's brand of ethical collectivism, based on a collective economy, where goods are commonly held rather than privately owned, falls flat amongst *most* Americans. Primarily because the nation enjoys a heritage of capitalism and individual liberties—such as "freedom of speech, freedom of religion, the right to private property, the right to earn and retain profit, and the right to emigrate"—that collectivized countries, such as Russia and Sweden, do not enjoy (Bernstein, The Freedom Gradient in Ayn Rand's Novels, 281). Since they either have a history of subordinating themselves to an authority figure, like a King, or a Pope, or they have a track record of valuing the collective masses over any individual citizen. But since America was never under the rule of a King, or a Pope, or mobs of degraded people who were out for blood—but instead has a proud history of individualism, selfishness, semi-autonomy, and localized rule—Toohey encounters firm resistance when he tries to collectivize the country. Since America's legacy of civil and economic freedoms, which are enforced by a strong legal system, makes it very difficult for Toohey to work his collectivist magic in the United States.

Consequently, because Ayn Rand highlights the difference between a nation where people are free to choose their "social bonds," versus a country where people are forced into different types of social relationships, she undercuts four different kinds of collectivists in *The Fountainhead*: (1) People who do not value for themselves, like Toohey's followers; (2) People who see the means as the end, like Gail Wynand; (3) People who conform their identities to other estimations, like Peter Keating; and (4) People, like Lois Cook, who place other people's beliefs before their own thinking. This, then, is why Ayn Rand criticizes people "who have lost [their] ability to value for themselves and [thus] accept, on faith or on someone [else's] authority, the opinions of others." (Journals, 91). Specifically, people, like Gail Wynand who deploy corrupt journalism for money and power because they "reverse the 'end' [for the] 'means,' "; people like Peter Keating who "exist only in the eyes of others, not in their own;" and people like Ellsworth Toohey, who form their ideas *not* because they believe in certain notions (Journals, 91). But because they know that others will support their opinions.

Ayn Rand also elevates the concept of individualism—over the concept of collectivism—by showing readers that people who value for themselves by thinking alone—like Howard Roark, for example, or Henry Cameron, for instance—create great works of high intellectual, moral, and spiritual worth. Whereas people who compromise their values by working in groups, like Peter Keating, produce sub-standard products. Textually, Ayn Rand illustrates this idea by not only having Peter Keating type conformists—who produce buildings in groups or committees—make abysmal flops of very little worth she also exemplifies this concept by having independent thinkers, like Roark and Cameron, create great buildings of high intellectual value. Textually, this is evident in action when we consider that when Keating designs toothpaste buildings during *The March of the Centuries World's Fair* [21] with 7 other architects he generates a disgusting hash of jumbled structures. Whereas when Cameron and Roark design the *Dana* and *Cortlandt* buildings *alone* they create esthetic skyscrapers of great substance. Indeed, the juxtaposition between pioneering buildings primarily alone versus conforming structures mainly in a group, shows readers that when a man produces works with other people the probable result of all his compromises, appeasements, and betrayals, is something quite bad. Whereas when an individual creates by himself and for himself he does better work than he can produce collectively. Because he only has himself to please. This contrast, in turn, between the products of individualists versus the products of collectivists harkens to Ayn Rand's main thesis that worthy creations are not the product of a great many men working together but rather that worthy creations are the creation of several independent men working alone. Also, by portraying the idea

---

[21]   Because **Keating,** and **seven other architects, work together** to design the *March of the Centuries* main buildings – "through conference after conference, each [yielding] to [the will] of others, in [a] true collective spirit, non trying to impose his selfish esthetic ideas" on the group – **they produce squiggly buildings that are extremely ugly** (587). Whereas **when Roark,** or Cameron, **design** the *Dana* or *Cortlandt* buildings **alone** they **produce great structures** of high esthetic worth. Since they are free to realize their own vision.

that excellent inventions are *mainly* produced alone, in solitary isolation, Ayn Rand shows readers that the "proper life is possible only when man *is* allowed (and encouraged, and taught, and practically forced) to live for himself" (Journals, 85).

Another theme Ayn Rand depicts in *The Fountainhead* is the connection between individualism, collectivism, and personal responsibility. To clarify this relationship, Ayn Rand shows readers that since individualists, like Roark, stand alone, think for themselves, and originate their own projects (almost singlehandedly) it is clear who is connected to the results of a given project, or to the consequence of a given idea. But when collectivists, like Toohey, undertake a certain project (in a group setting) or propound certain ideas (in a collectivized atmosphere) they make it nearly impossible for people to detect who is responsible for what undertaking; and, thus, who is accountable for backing certain concepts. Because in a group (or collective) setting, it is extremely difficult to unwind who thought of and gave form to a particular idea or project. Since it is the nature of collectivism (and by implication altruism) to so disperse responsibility that no one can be identified with it. This, then, is why many of Ayn Rand's characters shun being directly linked to a project in any meaningful way whatsoever. By forming group after group, committee after committee, collective after collective, in *The Fountainhead*. So they can dodge their basic responsibilities. Take, for example, Ellsworth Toohey. He not only forms the *Council of American Builders*, the *Council of American Artists*, and the *Council of American Writers*, he also forms the *Organization of Young Architects*, and scores of other groups, in the book. To dodge all culpability for the actions of the collective. Indeed, Toohey's glaring evasion of responsibility here, which he achieves by assuming an elegant intellectual disguise, highlights Ayn Rand's basic thesis: that when the originator of a given venture divorces himself from the consequences of that endeavor, the net result is the creation of a group, or collective environment, where members cannot be held accountable for the results of that group. This, then, is why Toohey is never chairman of any organization he leads. Because he wants to evade accountability for any actions that he takes. This is also why Toohey creates group after group in *The Fountainhead*. So he can tie all consequences to the group. So he can blame the group, if necessary, for espousing unpalatable ideas associated with his collectivist activities. Conversely, because Howard Roark is basically alone, while creating, he is not only responsible for the outcome of his ideas and undertakings he is also accountable for his projects. Because in Roark's world it is not only clear who is connected to a certain belief or a particular enterprise it is also clear who is responsible for originating a specific project. While in Toohey's world, responsibility for a set of ideas, or a series of actions, is assigned to a group, or to society, and thus to no one at all.

Ayn Rand also criticizes the types of second handers, like Toohey and Wynand, who do not form beliefs because others share them, but rather espouse a particular idea, because they know, *almost* by instinct, that others will believe in it. This is why they advocate "popular sayings [prevalent] in the American culture." [Such as] " 'image is everything' " [and] " 'perception is reality' " (Bernstein, Objectivism in One Lesson). In order to embrace the idea that social beliefs shape, then govern, the truth of the real world out there [22]. Said differently, because Toohey and Wynand swap what people believe is so for what is really so, they undercut the notion that reality exists whether a person can see it, or not. Indeed, Toohey and Wynand's drive to bend reality to their will, makes them, "the deadliest kind of second handers, [because] they are [meters] of the crowd" (Journals, 172). Since they approve of things not because they like them. But because they know they will become popular. This, then, is why these types of collectivists are taught to value popular approval and social esteem as a spiritual reward for their efforts on behalf of the mob. For they "claim that a man's higher values comes from his

---

[22] According to Ayn Rand, however, there is an objective, absolute, reality based on natural laws, that exists, whether a person can conceive it, or not. Since existence exists and reality is prime; while a consciousness can be conscious of that reality, or not. For instance, rational scientists, who have the acute use of their five senses—sight, hearing, smell, taste and touch—are connected to earthly reality. And, can choose to transmit, that reality, or not. Whereas neurotics, who are only semi-connected to reality, can only transmit that reality, sometimes. However, psychotics, like schizophrenics, are completely disconnected from reality. Thus, never, can they transmit reality at all. Except, maybe, if they take Objectivist coursework, for decades, and thus, rehabilitate themselves, so they are schizophrenics no more. But rather, become sane people, instead.

sense of [collective] honor before the mob" (Journals, 85). Derives from his sense that his collective brothers approve of everything he thinks, says, writes, and does. Here, Ayn Rand points out that Wynand like second-handers achieve success not by being who they are—nor by living out their highest values. But giving the masses what they want. So they can rule the crowd by writing articles that the multitude will sanction. Yet by not keeping himself apart from the crowds spiritually, Wynand corrupts himself internally by choosing to seek power over men. However, as Ayn Rand writes:

> when a man shifts the center of his life from his own ego to the opinions of others, when those others become the determining factor in all his higher values, when [his] higher values [are sacrificed] for money or physical gain, [and] when his ideals are one and his actual existence another—he is leading a second-hand life.

(Journals, 82)

This, then, is why mob-loving secondhanders, like Wynand, are usually media spin doctors, literary critics, or unprincipled politicians, of some sort, who express and mold the voice of public opinion, by writing and editing articles and speeches that transmit the values of the masses.

Ayn Rand also denounces conformists who follows others. Individuals who uncritically substitute the judgment of others in place of their own minds. Take *Peter Keating*, for example, he refuses to think for himself because he relies on society's beliefs to form his own convictions. Since he wants to win the crowd's approval by uncritically accepting what the group thinks is so. This *protean* shapeshifting makes Keating a "selfless" social chameleon who allows others to determine his career choice. This is why Keating not only chooses architecture rather than the field he loves—painting—this is also why he sacrifices his childhood love for Catherine Halsey to marry the boss's daughter, a woman named Dominique Francon whom he is actually afraid of. Because others will gape at and approve of her. Evidently, since Keating is completely dependent on others to form his own convictions, he copies *Roark's* work; fawns before all superiors; agrees with others; and obeys the crowd. Because he wants to win the sanction, the respect, and the consent of society for everything he says, thinks, and does. Because his life is thoroughly dominated by the public. Accordingly, Keating surrenders his mind to society so completely—to collectivized crowds of dull people so totally—since he blindly seeks to impress others by waving a false flag. By touting his fake achievements. Primarily, because he wants to fatten his wallet – glorify his person – and enhance his career – in whatever way he can. Nevermind that he does not deserve the social station that he has. That does not matter. What matters is that he advances his social standing by winning the reverence of strangers. Because it is enough for Keating to be "thought [of as] great—[not to actually] be great" (633). Yet since image is everything to Keating, while substance is nothing, he does not care that others respect him on false grounds. What matters to Keating is that others *think* he is great. Thus, Keating gives-up his mind to please the masses in whatever way he can. Since he thinks that if he can just steer the thoughts of others in his favor then he can gain the social respect that he so desperately wants. For Keating is a psychological manipulator of the highest order who employs a *Machiavellian* philosophy to trick people: "Always be what people want you to be. Then you've got them." (267). Yet, he was not always this way. During his childhood, for instance, Keating thinks and values independently. Because when Keating was young he has "selfish" values in his life that the crowds do not instill—like his passion for painting, for example, or his love of Catherine *Halsey*, for instance. Yet when he goes to school, begins to work, and becomes a respected member of society, Keating surrenders his mind to other people by abandoning all of his blooming passions. So he can please his mother, or placate *Ellsworth Toohey*, or satiate the masses more generally. This makes Keating a mindless conformist who betrays his inner soul to curry favor with the outer masses. For *cachet* and prestige. Thus, to get social respect, Keating is obediently compliant to the group and to high society. Since he feels that he can only get ahead in life by manipulating other people. Accordingly, Keating surrenders his mind to society so completely that it

their designs into a discordant mixture, he is an esthetic conformist of the first order, who gives up his own self to please others.

A last example of conformity (i.e. of elevating someone else's judgment above one's own) is *Guy Francon*, a traditional architect, who unbendingly adheres to a classical building style in order to harness the resurgence of classicism ushered in by the *March of the Centuries World's Fair*. After this large international exhibition, then, Francon is happy to comply with society's desire for buildings designed in a classical manner. Since Francon unthinkingly accepts the public's standards, values, and ideas as his own. Because he elevates the crowd's beliefs before his own identity. This, then, is why Francon passively surrenders his mind to appease the masses. Because he prefers to follow the will of others rather than to be guided by his own judgment and decisions. Ergo, Francon's desire to contort his identity by warping his buildings to please others ultimately makes him a secondhander who blindly accepts the ideas of his colleagues.

In brief, all of Ayn Rand's conformist characters willing abandon their own survival instruments—their minds—to gain social standing. To gain a positive social position that would otherwise be impossible for them to win on their own merits. Thus, these types of mindless conformists copy the thinking of their contemporaries. So they can dodge all responsibility for having their own motivations. Since, on their own, these second-raters are intellectually and morally bankrupt. Because they do not create original, valuable ideas, of their own making to advance their lives. Rather, they look to others for guidance.

Most importantly, actual real-life examples of this type of blind conformity shows readers that people who choose to be guided by others, instead of following their own lights, harm themselves and their lives.

For example, the real world abounds with examples of unprincipled social climbers a la Peter Keating. People who reach the height of a company **not** by producing substantive work products but by engaging in clever interpersonal manipulation (i.e. wheedling office politics). These character-types are ultimately uncritical conformists. Since they **do not** build their careers by means of excellent work performance. Rather, they seek to climb a social power ladder by winning over their superiors with *fulsome* flattery [23]. Thus, to rise-up in a company without really trying, second-raters, like Peter Keating, first assume the beliefs of their important co-workers and bosses. Then they direct these people's ideas back to them by regurgitating what their superiors and colleagues said to them previously. So they can climb to the commanding heights of an organization by means of role-playing and *gamesmanship*, instead of ascending the ranks of a company by being good at their jobs and speaking the truth to power.

Another real-world example of conformity is the student who wants to be a literary critic, yet betrays his deep-seated values, because his family pressures him into a more lucrative field, like the law, for example. He, too, betrays himself, by being guided by the judgment of others instead of being guided by his own rulings.

Yet another example of conformity relates to people who follow cult leaders, like *David Koresh*, since they need to identify with a peer group. Since they need to be led by a charismatic leader who will fill the vacuum of their personalities with a faith of his own. With a toxic ideology that they can relate to, embrace, and spread. Because they need to believe in something. Thus, since new-cultists lack a strong personality to begin with, they do not develop and pursue their own passions independently. Rather, they are generally open to subliminal suggestion; to mind control; to being brain-washed by a cult guru.

Vacillating politicians, like *George Bush* Senior, are also conformists because they abandon their principles when public opinion polls reveal their morals to be unpopular. This is why Bush reversed his pro-choice stand that he formed in the 1970's when he was a Congressional candidate, so he could adopt a position more acceptable to the mainstream of his party. To get elected. Thus, Bush flip-flopped on abortion, and a number

---

[23] Here, Ayn Rand asks **"what"** status-mongering **second-handers**, like Peter Keating, **"get in exchange for giving up the reality of their work and of their lives?"** (Journals, 85). **What**, in other words, **do they gain "by spending their lives at a *second-hand*" job**, a job "secondary to their real purpose," a job "which is only a means to an end" (Journals, 85). **The answer is nothing** really. Because they give up their primary identity and original purpose in return for an expected future benefit, like money, derived from the crowd's approval.

of other issues, in his run up to his presidency, to get more votes. Since he relied on public opinion polls, not his own conscience, to define his positions.

Another type of real-life secondhander are people who not only equate their own value with how much money they have relative to other people but people who also measure their own personal success *only* in terms of their net-worth. These types of second-raters, then, may feel jealous if one of their neighbors has a bigger house, or a fancier car, or a newer tennis court, then he does. Accordingly, he might tear down his house to build a residence bigger than his neighbor's; or purchase a new car better than his neighbor's; or build a tennis court that is superior to what is next door. Because he "wants to keep up with the Jones's."

Penultimately, another type of real-world secondhander, according to Bernstein, is the young person who takes drugs—even though he, or she, knows that substance abuse is dangerous to them because it damages their health, and jeopardizes their life—simply to please their friends. So they can fit into a peer group. So they can be cool by taking mind altering chemicals.

One last example of a real-life conformist are individuals who choose their romantic partners not based on intellectual agreement, philosophic mutuality, and a sense-of-life affinity. But rather individuals who choose a spouse because of who their families and friends approve of. Because the suitor makes a lot of money, or comes from a good background, or is of the right class, or age, or is respected socially—or all of these qualities. Thus, these types of conformists date and marry people because they are rich, or socially connected, or come from the upper classes, instead of merging with a "soul-mate" because that person makes them happy by sharing their values. Instead, these types of second-raters give-up their romantic happiness by marrying a person who lacks the beliefs, the principles, and the standards required to forge the bonds of a joyful relationship.

All of these people, and numerous others, are real-life conformists who not only allow the dominant beliefs of society (or their families) to control them but also exist as followers, in one form, or another. Because they choose to obey others rather than to be led by their own evaluations and decisions.

Similarly, another category of collectivist Ayn Rand criticizes in *The Fountainhead* are *Lois Cook* type non-conformists who seek to discover what society values in order to shock its members through rebellion. So they can collect admission for their stunts [24]. Thus, rebels, like Lois Cook, oppose the precepts of the general culture as a strategy to make money from the ensuing public scandal, (i.e. from the resultant fallout). So they can enrich themselves by exciting and entertaining the crowd by lampooning civilizational norms. Accordingly, real world agitators like Lois Cook also want to "throw sweat in the faces" of the popular culture because they also need to define their identities by mocking a country's standards, values, and judgments, *writ small*, as a method of rejecting the world's values, *writ large*. (245). So they can make themselves feel better than others for being clever enough to trick people—whom they view as suckers—out of their hard earned money. Because by opposing realistic art, non-conformists like Lois *Cook* feel proud for their cunning wits. Feel pleased for bamboozling society with their artistic con games and valueless creations. For in the microcosm of Ayn Rand's literary universe, which corresponds to the macrocosm of the real world, Lois Cook is a *Dadaist* (or absurdist) writer in the style of a *James Joyce*, or a *Gertrude Stein*, who composes her books in an "unintelligible writing style, [that] is a deliberate assault on the rules of grammar and meaning" (Bernstein, Cliff's Notes, 116). Because Cook, like Stein, is also an American cubist who purposefully writes books in an incomprehensible writing style consisting of "incoherent sentences in which words are related by sound and emotional association, not by an [effort] to communicate [thought and] meaning" (Bernstein, Cliff's Notes, 116). Similarly, not only does Lois Cook violate the rules of good grammar in her writing; she also violates the rules of clean hygiene in her personal grooming. Since she does not shower often, which ultimately causes her "hair [to hang] about her ears in greasy strands" (244). Similarly, because Cook never cuts

---

[24] In this regard, Lois Cook is "an exhibitionist who [is] being different as a stunt, as a lark, just to attract attention to [herself. A racketeer who] "oppose[s] the crowd and amuses it and collects admission to the side show" (54).

(or files) her nails, "her fingernails [are] broken" like the cracked talons of a falcon (244). Besides violating social beliefs in beauty and writing, Cook also mocks what other people believe are good living quarters. By instructing Keating to build her "a living room without windows," in her *Bowery* townhouse, when most people want to let light and air into their homes through large windows, so they can see and breath better (245). This is also why Lois has "Kerosene [horse] carriage' lamps," in her townhouse (245). Instead of electricity. So she can get a rise out of people. Even though Kerosene lamps char walls; create excess heat; are slightly smelly; and require *copious* amounts of time, labor, and energy, to install and maintain. Similarly, to further shock people, Lois wants a "black ceiling" in her domicile, so her chambers look cramped and dark, when *most* people value white ceilings in their houses, to make their rooms feel spacious and bright (245). Similarly, to stun, Lois Cook wants a "tile floor" in her living room, when most people either install carpets in their parlors – to absorb sound – or put hard wood floors in their lounges – to ease cleaning (245). Because wood floors are easier to clean and harder to damage. But because Lois Cook constantly opposes the standards of others to extract the public's wealth, she wants her "house to be *ugly*; magnificently ugly; the ugliest house in *New York*" (245). So she can gain further notoriety by making a *ludicrous* spectacle of herself—just like a circus ring master tries to shock his viewers with bearded ladies, retarded midgets, and other sundry freaks, that pierce and display their genitalia. For Lois Cook believes that she should "surpass [people who] work hard to achieve beauty by throwing their sweat in their face[s]; by destroying them at one stroke, [by] be[ing] Gods; by being ugly" (245). This, in short, is how *Cook* maintains a dominant position in the *slime-light* of popular scandal. By elevating the power of destruction and ugliness over the power of construction and beauty. For all *Cook* can do is destroy other people's values by being ugly; not build her own values by being beautiful. Thus, although nonconformists like Lois Cook appear to be staunch individualists, they are social collectivists, really, since they pit their values against what society believes is moral. For the non-conformist's truth is not only social it is the opposite of what other people believe. Ergo, because Lois Cook merely *opposes* what other people think is sacred instead of judging what is good, or bad, for herself, ultimately, she has a collectivist's soul. Because she elevates other people's beliefs before her own thinking. Since her ideological beginning point is the beliefs of others. This, then, is how Lois Cook shows readers that if a person's primary orientation in life is a rejection of the world's values, through an unthinking rebuff of other people's judgment, then they too are collectivists, in spirit, not individualists, in essence. Because they also define their identities not by following, like Peter Keating does, but by rejecting social values instead, like Lois Cook does.

A real-life example of a Lois Cook type non-conformist is *Lady Gaga*, a name that purposefully rhymes with *DaDa*, since she, just like Cook, is a ludicrous popular artist who poses for the crowd, by performing various stunts to amuse the masses. For instance, she wore a "meat-dress" to the 2010 MTV music awards, to display her rebellion against America's fashion values. By dressing so unconventionally, *Lady Gaga* shows us that she is a "posturing nonconformist" like Lois Cook who seeks to hurt others by undermining their values. Since her crazy clothes, bizarre hair dos, thumping beats, and defiant lyrics, conveys a staunch refusal to conform to prevailing social customs and practices as a rule. Not because she is an individual who does her own thing regardless of what the popular thing to do is. But because she first wants to discover the values of mainstream society, so she can later reject them through her person and music.

In sum, what is important here, is that "neither the conformist nor the non-conformist permits his own understanding of reality to serve as the cognitive compass or guiding element of his life. In both cases, the principles of other men—whether to embrace or reject them—are [his] ruling consideration (Bernstein, Objectivism in One Lesson, 76).

But because Roark is neither a rebel, like Lois Cook, nor a follower, like Peter Keating, but rather is an individualist thinker who relies on his own judgement to form his own conclusions, he explodes the false dichotomy between conformity and nonconformity. The wrong alternative between being like a Lois Cook versus being like a Peter Keating. For Roark is an active thinker, who is a producer and creator, not a passive copier, who is a mimic and imitator. This makes Roark a first-hander who relies on his own volition—not the values of others—to form his own conclusions. Such an "independent [man, then] is not concerned with what others think—neither to obey nor to defy them; rather, he is concerned with what he thinks." (Bernstein, Cliff's Notes, 35). So he can pursue his own values. Because, after all, "a man's self," Bernstein remind us, "is his mind, [is] his thinking, [is] the judgement he deploys to choose his personal values" (Bernstein, Objectivism in One Lesson, 61). And if he betrays these values to please others then he "surrenders more than his values to others: he betrays his judgment (i.e. the thinking by which he formed those values)" (Bernstein, Objectivism in One Lesson, 89).

Thus, deep-thinkers, like *Roark*, explode the standard understanding that people are either conformists or nonconformists. By showing readers that they have a third option in life. To be independent thinkers who reach their own conclusions by cogitating carefully. By pondering the outer world, by reflecting on nature, and by dissecting metaphysical reality, to observe their own truth, according to natural laws, just like Roark does. So they can also form, then enact, their own value judgements, as our hero-protagonist does. For Roark does not copy, or mock, the works of previous minds for a fleeting social sanction. Rather, *Roark* looks to facts, looks to evidence, and looks to his own mind to perceive reality. To perceive a worldly truth that governs what he does and who he will become in life. He does not undermine his identity and goals in exchange for social approval.

Similarly, original thinkers, to Ayn Rand, are like Roark. Because they are also independent men who autonomously recognize an idea's truth by means of examining the external world. By means of deploying their logic. As opposed to the thoughtless acceptance, or rejection, of other people's values, based on the feelings of someone like a Peter Keating, or based on the emotionalism of someone like a Lois Cook. This, then, is why *Roark* follows his own truth by relying on his own mind to form and direct the course of his life. As opposed to pursuing the public's truth, like Peter Keating, or rejecting the public's truth, like Lois Cook. This makes Roark *neither* a conformist, who voluntarily gives up his mind to others, nor a nonconformist, who uncritically rejects the standards of others to *galvanize* the masses. Rather, Roark shows readers that a third option is possible for them—to be an individualist thinker who forms, and defends, his own values by exercising his independent volition.

Further, to disassociate traditional collectivist principles, like compassion, sympathy, and *pathos*, from interpersonal virtue, Ayn Rand strips *Altruism* of the positive connotations historically associated with it. Not only to destroy the sympathetic landmarks traditionally connected to this selfless ideology but also to deconstruct *Altruism's* popular reception in the general culture. She does this by showing readers that compassion is **not** always such a positive emotion to feel. Since sympathy (to her) does not always mean that a person is benevolently concerned for the well-being and misfortunes of others. To her compassion is wrong because: One, it makes a man sacrifice his own greater values—his money, health, and time—for a lesser value, or a complete non-value—like helping total strangers. Two, it prompts a man to exchange what is more important to him for that which is less important (or not important at all) to him. Three, it degrades a man's fundamental dignity by making him rely on the pity and alms of others to survive instead of on his own mind. Four, it *can* lead to looking down on others because they are repugnant in some way. Five, it justifies the suffering of others as a means by which a person can exercise their own virtue. And, six, "it may distract one from the use of the mind by a substitution of feeling." (Den Uyl, P). Thus, to emphasize the natural concern an individual should have for their own values and identity—while also stressing how harmful it is to have a "sacrificial" concern for others welfare—Ayn Rand has her mouthpiece character, one *Dominque Francon*, sarcastically say to a woman named *Mrs. Jones*, thus:

> You've met Mr. Roark, Mrs. Jones? And you didn't like him? Oh, he's the type of man for whom one can feel no compassion? How true. Compassion is a wonderful thing. It's what one feels when one looks at a squashed caterpillar. An elevating experience. One can let oneself go and spread—you know, like taking a girdle off. You don't have to hold your stomach,

your heart or your spirit up—when you feel compassion. All you have to do is look down. It's much easier. When you look up, you get a pain in the neck. Compassion is the greatest virtue. It justifies suffering. There's got to be suffering in the world, else, how would we be virtuous and feel compassion? Oh, it has an antithesis—but such a hard, demanding one. Admiration, Mrs. Jones, admiration. But that takes more than a girdle. So I say that anyone for whom we can't feel sorry is a vicious person. Like Howard Roark.

(288)

Dominique says this to undercut the idea that a person is only worthy and likable if others can feel sorry for them because they are pathetic and pitiable in some way. She also says this to refute the idea that a person is only valuable if they suffer because they are poor, or diseased, or handicapped, or disabled, or are unfortunate, in some other way. Most importantly, Ayn Rand indicates, in the above passage, that the average man can "achieve the moral stature of a Howard Roark, by practicing the opposite of compassion: the demanding virtue of admiration" (Ghate).

Thus, to dissolve the associative link between virtue and sympathy in the minds of her readers, Ayn Rand shows her audience, through Dominique Francon, that integrity and empathy are not causally related. Because being honest, and having strong moral principles, does not mean that one necessarily understands and shares the feelings of others. What it does mean is that a person can admire [25], respect, and emulate another person, because they are great. But because exercising such feelings of admiration would prohibit *Mrs. Jones* from enacting her ultimate value of *Altruism*—by exercising her primary virtue of compassion—she does not look up to great others. Rather, she looks down on the poor, the lame, the halt, and the blind, to feel better about herself. Instead of showing

---

[25] As Ghate reminds us, "To practice the virtue of admiration does demand much of a man. [Because] he must respect and nurture the best within himself and within any man. [Since] to practice the virtue of admiration is to stand, head lifted, and give thanks for the greatness of another man and all that it, and its sight, will make possible in one's own life." (Ghate).

people that they can be strong and should be strong. That, in a word, they need not suffer. Yet she fails to realize that in a world dominated by altruism—or an undiscriminating sympathy for others—individuals not only lose sight of themselves by constantly immersing themselves in other people's problems. But they also diminish their own self-respect by internalizing the indiscriminate suffering of others. Since depravity, under *Altruism*, can be seen as a natural condition of all human beings—to a greater or lesser extent. Because when we constantly identify with and absorb the hopeless suffering of unfortunate people, we ultimately lose respect for ourselves and for the human race. Since blind feelings of humanitarian sympathy eventually undermines the admiration we should have for ourselves and for distinguished others. This is why Ayn Rand infers that pitying others because they suffer ultimately undercuts our own identities. Since pitying others instead of objectively judging them ultimately undercuts the primary role that reason and rationality and logic should play in our professional and personal lives. Because "the mind is more critical to our humanity than our emotions." (Den Uyl).

But it is this type of anti-mind emotionalism, reasons Ayn Rand, that ultimately makes readers see a "less attractive side of altruism—a side that stands in the way of the virtues she wishes to promote," (Integrity, independence, self-reliance, and rationality). (Den Uyl, 82). For modern society, to Ayn Rand, is largely corrupted by the sentimental elements of "connective sympathy," which, to her, no longer means a neutral concern for the well-being of others who are important to us. But rather is the elevation of others social welfare at the cost of our own goals, meaning, and purpose. Thus, Ayn Rand intentionally divorces the traditional definition of empathy from her literature to highlight the need of people to break cleanly with the vulgar sentimentality of modern life. So they can destroy the role of corrupting emotions from their lives. Which, to her, is the only way they can live a happy life.

Evidently, Ayn Rand reverses traditional definitions of compassion and sympathy in *The Fountainhead* by not only showing readers that the connective qualities of compassion, rarely, if ever, coincides with goodness and virtue, but also by excluding all selfless concerns from human behavior. By denying the idea that people should organize themselves along altruistic lines.

To realize this aim, Ayn Rand shows readers that the process by which an unselfishness idealist, such as *Catherine Halsey*, becomes a cynical nihilist, such as Ellsworth Toohey, is precisely through *Altruism*. By believing in and exercising it.

To explain, thanks to Catherine's altruistic social work [26], which demands that she live for others and place others above herself, she ends up hating poor people in her later life. When before she loved the indigent. However, after decades of selflessly serving society, she no longer believes that poor people are dignified individuals who simply need a helping hand up because they cannot hack it on their own. Rather, after being a social worker for many years Catherine changes into a mean-spirited tyrant who actually hates the people she is supposed to be helping. For practicing *Altruism* for so long has transformed Catherine's initial will to help the impoverished into an intense dislike of poor people. Thus, because she gives up her own selfish values in life, Catherine becomes patronizably cruel to poor people when initially she was not.

Because after Catherine is a day nursery attendant at the *Clifford Settlement House*; then *The Social Director* for the *Children's Occupational Therapy Unit* at the *Stoddard Home*, followed by a minor-bureaucrat in Washington D.C., she is no longer the high-minded optimist that she once was. Rather, she *transmogrifies* herself from a starry-eyed idealist who wants to aid the needy into a small-minded bigot who is no longer a benevolent benefactress. For "having been taught selflessness for years, Catherine begins to give up her sense of idealism, and the resulting decline is noticeable. Earlier in the story, Keating had observed that Catherine, at the time almost twenty, 'looked no older than she had looked at seventeen' (83). Later, after years of social work and Toohey, we are told that at twenty-six 'she looked like a woman trying to hide the fact

---

26   When asked about her low opinion of social workers, Ayn Rand replied that though she is "opposed to the collectivist-altruist kind of social worker (like Katie from *The Fountainhead*) [it] doesn't mean that all social workers are frustrated little tyrants. [Because] there are good and bad [people] in every profession. (Rand, *Answers*, 122).

of being over thirty' " (359). (Bayer). Indeed, Catherine looks haggard, precisely because she gave up all of her personal values in life to become a compassionate social worker. Yet by practicing the selfless philosophy of altruism, Catherine "becomes [so] unhappy—in such a horrible, nasty, undignified, unclean, and dishonest way"— that she ultimately undermines (through her person) the notion that "one can only find true happiness [in life] by dedicating oneself to others" (372). Because years-and-years of "sorting Toohey's mail, filing his press clippings, answering his fan letters, and making his scrapbook," coupled with a soul-crushing career in social work, strips Catherine of her own self-respect (i.e. her own personal, selfish, values in life) (Gurgen, 23). Because by filling her days with Toohey's disvalues, instead of living out her own life according to her own identity, Catherine ultimately loses herself. By denying her basic character.

To explain, after Catherine adopts her uncle's *toxic* ideology that "unhappiness comes from selfishness," she renounces everything that makes her happy in life. Like her love for Peter Keating, for example, or her desire to enroll in college, for instance. Yet when she was young and in love with Peter Keating, and, thus, saw him often during her early days, Catherine wanted to "kiss every ragged kid on her block" (374). However, because her uncle Ellsworth (else-worth) strips Catherine of her individuality by ensuring that she neither marries the man she loves, as she had always wanted, nor goes to college, as she had always desired, Catherine begins to *abhor* the people that she once set out to help. Therefore, now "she resents [people] who find lives for themselves, as they remind her of her own abandoned college ambitions." (Bayer). Thus, by denying all of her selfish values in life at Toohey's behest, Catherine represses herself so completely that she suppresses her best self. Which, in turn, not only makes her lose touch with the reality of her person and situation but which ultimately diminishes her respect for others. For Catherine's initial drive to help people through social work is replaced by her uncle Ellsworth's altruistic philosophy of selflessness. Since Toohey steals Catherine's soul by destroying all of her selfish values in life.

Thus, after years of social work Catherine begins to disbelieve the idea that people are entitled to the free use of their own minds. For she resents it when people under her care disagree with her. Since multiple decades of supporting the lame, the halt, the blind, and the retarded [27], makes her doubt that human beings know what is good for them. That people can be strong, should be strong, and are strong. Catherine feels this way primarily because she has little exposure—in social work—to noble souls who are better than the people she typically encounters.

Thus, after pursuing a career in soul-destroying social work for so long, Catherine tells a slum woman that she does not "appreciate what social workers [do] for trash like her" (373). Even though Catherine cries for hours afterwards, since she cannot believe how unkind she is becoming, she still cannot help it that she starts to actually hate people, when in her early days she truly loved people. Ergo, by instilling in his niece an altruistic philosophy of suffering and hopelessness, Toohey ensures that she does not have anything of her own to live for anymore.

However, Catherine is also to blame for her downfall. Because she allowed her uncle to drain away the most important aspects of herself (i.e. her fundamental identity) instead of standing her ground by being who she is. Regardless of his criticisms. Thus, Catherine is also culpable for allowing Toohey to deprive her of her spirit. For enabling Toohey to turn her into a lesser version of himself—a clone who follows her uncle's marching orders to a tee—with blind obedience and total subordination. Hence, Catherine is also accountable for not knowing who she is anymore; for not knowing what she wants anymore; for not knowing how to realize her aims. Since everybody, Ayn Rand reminds us, has a self-made soul that determines what decisions they will make in life; that governs who they will become in this world; that guides and directs the course of their lives. Sadly, Catherine loses sight of this reality because she gives-up her own active role in forming her own being. Ergo, because Catherine is mad at herself for sacrificing her soul to Toohey—instead of

---

[27] Catherine's embittered experiences with congenitally deformed people—individuals who can't see, or hear, or smell, or touch, or cogitate—makes her forget that people who are born with physical and mental deformities are in no way to blame for their maladies. For Catherine's social work clouds her view that a person's in-born traits are completely beyond their control.

making her own way in life—she vents her Toohey anger on her wards in a very nasty way.

To explain, since Catherine never married a very handsome Peter Keating when she was young – because Toohey convinces her not to – she is furious when a girl in her charge happily marries a very attractive boy despite her counsel not to. She is mad at this development because Catherine does not like to be reminded that she never married her true love as she should have. Because her uncle convinced her not to. Similarly, because Toohey also strips his niece of her career ambitions, Catherine grows enraged when one of her wards finds a good job all by herself, without Catherine's help. Here, Catherine is furious, since she followed what her uncle wanted for her, instead of creating a unique career for herself by following her own vision. Thus, because Catherine betrayed herself for Toohey, she now feels that she must inflict her own pain onto others.

Evidently, now Catherine wants to wreak her own hurt, frustrations, and disappointments onto innocent others, like her wards. Because she now feels that if she can't be happy, other people have no right to be. This is why Catherine thinks that she must also strip other people of their own unique identities by depriving them of their personal values, just like Toohey did to her. Thus, in her later life, Catherine functions like Toohey. By projecting her self-denying experiences with Toohey onto others. So she can ultimately destroy other people's lives just as Toohey destroyed hers. Thereby, inflicting her deep pain (i.e. her spiritual wounds) onto the general culture.

Thus, by the end of the novel, Catherine loses touch with herself so completely that she no longer questions the morality of her behavior as she did earlier. Since she swaps all of her former high-minded ideals for Toohey's *Marxist* philosophy. Because by the time Catherine becomes a minor DC bureaucrat she no longer advocates the moving principles that she once did. Rather, by novel's end, Catherine loses herself so completely—with the reality of her person and situation so thoroughly— that she becomes a "frustrated little tyrant" who issues "mean little orders from a venomous petulant mouth" (Rand, Answers, 122; Gurgen, 23). This is why she commands Keating to not order coffee at Thorpe's café, as he wants to, but to eat a fresh watercress salad instead, with no bread. This is also why Catherine says that private architects, like Peter Keating, have a moral obligation to "do a job not just for private profit and a fat fee, but with an [overarching] social purpose" in mind (622). Specifically, to give "a little time to government work [and to mankind's] broader [social] objectives," instead of just "money grubbing" (622). Further, she belittles anyone who does not live in Washington DC by saying that she wonders how "people can live anywhere other" than the federal capital (622). Because "Washington is the only grown-up place in the country" (622). Evidently, Catherine thinks that anybody other than a socially minded state-citizen—who sacrifices themselves to a service culture—is a *callow* human being. A juvenile child who should know when to shut their mouths and follow orders. This, then, is why Catherine not only "wants to be thanked for her service to the poor [this is also why] she only likes the poor who are servile to her." (Bayer). Because, to her, it is simply "impossible to make laymen understand the methods" of benevolent altruists like her, who know what is best for them (622-623). Since, when confronted by sage advice, these puerile babies, in Catherine's view, just utter stupid, boring complaints, when they should close their mouths and follow her edicts without question. Here, Catherine thinks that other people are not entitled to their own values, their own minds, their own ideas, and their own philosophies, even if those thoughts differ from what authoritarian bullies like her think is best for them. For thanks to her uncle Toohey's damaging sway, Catherine loses touch with the reality of her soul—i.e. with the actuality of her moral life—which ultimately ruins her existence. Thus, Catherine's fall from grace is an admonitory story that warns readers against the altruistic doctrine of living for others by placing others above ourselves. Because:

> the story of Catherine Halsey provides a [tragic] example— and a cautionary tale. After she surrenders every personal value—her education, her prospective marriage, her ambition—to serve her uncle, Ellsworth Toohey, and join his "humanitarian" cause, she subsists in a hollow state, an empty, bitter husk, which had once contained a vibrantly

innocent soul. [Because] the selfless surrender of one's values, [Catherine shows] logically necessitates the draining of all that provides meaning in one's life, [without which a] miserably unfulfilled existence inexorably follows.

(Bernstein, Objectivism in One Lesson, 13-14)

Said differently, by novel's end, Catherine betrays herself so fully that she completely corrupts her former innocence. Since by the *terminus* of the book, her innocent, simple nature is despoiled by the *Altruistic* philosophy of her uncle *Ellsworth Toohey*.

In sum, Catherine's tragic fall shows readers that Rand does not regard altruism as an innocent doctrine of kindness and goodwill. Rather, she feels that altruism is a vicious doctrine designed to purge people from what is best within them. Since altruism, to Rand, is not just the doctrine of placing others before self but of giving others moral *priority* over self.

Lastly, to shift the focus away from collectivists who live by the opinions of others, to individualists, who live by the work of their own mind, Ayn Rand changed the title of her book from *Second Hand Lives* to *The Prime Mover* followed by *Main Spring*, and finally *The Fountainhead*. In order to feature Howard Roark, not Peter Keating, as central to her book. So she could show readers that creators, egoists, and original beings are responsible for the advancements of modern civilization, while collectivists, imitators, and altruists, are to blame for society's social harms.

In conclusion, in *The Fountainhead* "Rand considers the conflict between the individual and the collective to be between those who would subordinate the individual to society (the collectivists) and those who see individuals as independent actors with the right to exist for their own sake (the individualists)" (Den Uyl, 32). In considering this opposition, Ayn Rand shows readers that a country's "political system either supports or impedes a person's quest to realize the best within them. In a free society upholding individual rights, a person is at liberty to pursue his dreams; in a totalitarian state where individual rights are crushed, he or she does as the state dictates." (Younkins, Introduction, 7). But in the comparatively free society of *The Fountainhead* individuals are free to make their own way in life by forming and maintaining their own identities. Since in the universe of the novel there is not much by way of state interference, or governmental impediments, that blocks characters from realizing their own values and identities. But in the relatively restricted society of the fictional dictatorships that Ayn Rand pictured in her novels, people residing under the collectivist governments of her books are not free to live out who they are. Since their rights are collectivized, then their identities are subsumed, by a *hermetic* state that brutally represses people's fundamental values and spirit. Conversely, Ayn Rand's individualist characters, such as Howard Roark, or Henry Cameron, create and thrive in a free country such as the *United States*. Because in America individual citizens retain most of the fundamental rights upheld by the nation's founders. While citizens who are ruled by a *Socialist, Marxist,* or *Communist* government are cruelly repressed by an all-pervasive state.

REFERENCES

Bayer, J.B. (2007). The Fountainhead and the Spirit of Youth. (pp.227-242). In Essays on Ayn Rand's the Fountainhead. Ed. Robert Mayhew. Lanham, MD: Lexington Books.

Berliner, M.S. (Ed). (1995). *Letters of Ayn Rand.* New York City, New York: Penguin Books.

Bernstein, A. (2000). *Cliff's Notes on Rand's The Fountainhead.* New York: Houghton Mifflin Harcourt.

Bernstein, A. (2016). *The Freedom Gradient in Ayn Rand's Novels.* (pp.279-286). In Capitalism and Commerce in Imaginative Literature: Perspectives on Business from Novels and Plays. Ed. Edward W. Younkins. Lanham, MD: Lexington Books.

Bernstein, A. (2008). *Objectivism in One Lesson: An Introduction to the Philosophy of Ayn Rand.* Lanham Maryland: Hamilton Books.

Burns, J. (2009). *Goddess of the Market: Ayn Rand and the American Right.* New York: Oxford U.P.

Den-Uyl. D. (1950). *The Fountainhead: An American Novel.* New York: Twayne Publishers.

Ghate, O. (2007). *The Basic Motivation of the Creator and the Masses in The Fountainhead.* (pp.243-283). In Essays on Ayn Rand's the Fountainhead. Ed. Robert Mayhew. Lanham, MD: Lexington Books.

Gurgen, Emre (2021). *The Fountainhead Reference Guide: A to Z (Narrative Version 2nd Edition)*. Illinois: AuthorHouse.

Harriman, D. (Ed.) (1999). *Journals of Ayn Rand*. New York: Plume.

Rand, A. & Mayhew, R. (Ed.). (2005). *Ayn Rand Answers: The Best of Her Q & A*. New York: New American Library.

Rand, A. (2016). *The Fountainhead*. New York: New American Library.

Schwartz, P. & Podritske, M. (Eds.) (2009). *Objectively Speaking: Ayn Rand Interviewed*. New York: Lexington Books.

Younkins, E. (2016). *Introduction to Capitalism and Commerce in Imaginative Literature: Perspectives on Business from Novels and Plays*. (pp.1-14) Ed. Edward W. Younkins. Lanham, MD: Lexington Books.

INDEX

Symbols

$500 check 91, 112

A

Albanian 7
Alexander Hamilton 47
Altruism 3, 9, 136, 148, 149, 150, 151, 152, 156
America 1, 6, 9, 18, 19, 26, 35, 38, 40, 46, 47, 53, 54, 55, 57, 117, 126, 128, 130, 131, 132, 133, 134, 146, 157
American citizen 12, 40, 48
American dream 18
American literature 3, 53
Americans xxvii, 1, 2, 3, 4, 5, 6, 7, 8, 9, 10, 11, 12, 13, 15, 17, 18, 19, 20, 21, 24, 25, 26, 27, 33, 34, 35, 36, 38, 39, 40, 41, 42, 43, 44, 46, 47, 48, 49, 50, 51, 53, 54, 55, 57, 58, 86, 121, 124, 125, 131, 133, 134, 136, 137, 144, 159, 160
Aquitania Hotel 60, 93, 94, 95, 96, 115
arc-welder 11
Atlantic Ocean 41
Austen Heller 46, 91, 103, 104, 112, 124, 131, 140
authoritarian autocracy 49
automobiles 17, 97

B

Banner 85, 101, 126, 127, 128, 129
Bassett Brush Company 129
Benjamin Franklin 47
billboards 4
Bill of Rights 40, 47
blue-collared 12, 18
Bostonian 88
Bowery 145
Brass 69, 92
building trades 11, 12, 19, 36, 74, 80, 91, 92, 105, 110, 118
Bulgarian 7
businessmen 2, 4, 130
business plan 15, 106

C

Caleb Bradley 117
Cameron 23, 24, 25, 44, 45, 72, 73, 90, 104, 109, 129, 135, 157
capitalism xxvii, 13, 19, 122, 123, 124, 125, 126, 127, 128, 129, 133, 134, 159, 160
Capitalism xxvii, 13, 19, 122, 123, 124, 125, 126, 127, 128, 129, 133, 134, 159, 160
capitalistic 18, 124, 125, 127, 129
capitalists 18, 113, 124, 125, 126, 127, 130
career 11, 20, 21, 23, 26, 38, 48, 51, 52, 65, 66, 72, 81, 87, 90, 93, 105, 106, 107, 108, 111, 114, 119, 138, 139, 141, 152, 153, 154

F

fascist 131, 132
Federalist 47
federated 13
Florida 117
French 7, 22, 74

G

Gail Wynand 36, 37, 46, 59, 79, 100,
    103, 104, 123, 125, 134
George Bush 142
George Mason 47
George Washington 47
Georgia Plantation 113, 114
German 7, 37
goods and services 16, 17, 18, 19, 125
Gothic 111, 113, 140
governmental 9, 100, 129, 157
Gowan's Gas Station 88, 103
Grand Canyon 41, 42
great American novel 27, 53, 54, 55
Greek 7, 112, 114
Gus Webb 94, 129
Guy Francon 90, 94, 103, 107, 108,
    109, 115, 141

H

Harford Times 4
Hearst Papers 6
Hebrew 7
The Heller House 10, 103, 112
Hell's Kitchen 46, 48
Henry Cameron 23, 24, 25, 44, 72, 90,
    104, 109, 135, 157
homo economicus 13
Howard Roark xxvii, 1, 4, 6, 10, 19,
    26, 36, 37, 39, 40, 52, 59, 60, 61,
    62, 63, 64, 76, 80, 94, 99, 100,
    103, 119, 125, 131, 135, 137, 149,
    156, 157

Hudson 40, 41, 115
Hudson River 41, 115
Hummer 70

I

Icelandic 7
Ideological 4, 5, 32, 113, 131, 132, 146
illiberal democracies 49
Indiana 4
Individualism xxvii, 1, 3, 4, 5, 6, 9, 39,
    53, 54, 55, 123, 124, 127, 129,
    130, 133, 134, 135, 136
Individual Rights 9, 19, 46, 47, 49, 131,
    133, 156
industrial 17
Industry 8, 13, 27, 75, 77, 92, 126
International 6, 141
I Swim With the Current 85, 129
Italian 7

J

James Madison 47
James Monroe 47
Janer's Department Store 82, 93,
    103, 117
janitors 11
Janss-Stuart Real Estate Company
    52, 113
Japanese 7
Jimmy Gowan 113, 124
Jimmy Kearns 127
John Adams 47
John C. Gall 4
John Erick Synte 88, 94, 111
John Erik Synte 91, 115
John Jay 47
journalists 4, 46, 49, 51, 54, 59, 60, 86,
    103, 106, 124, 125, 130
Jules Fougler 127
juris prudence 8
jurors 8, 9, 10

Printed in the United States
by Baker & Taylor Publisher Services